planning your
pension

planning your
pension

sue ward

KOGAN
PAGE

Dedicated to the memory of Dr Ruth Elliott

First published in 2002

Kogan Page Ltd
120 Pentonville Road
London N1 9JN
www.kogan-page.co.uk

© Sue Ward, 2002

British Library Cataloguing in Publication Data

A CIP record for this book is available from the British Library

ISBN 0 7494 3605 0

Typeset by Saxon Graphics Ltd, Derby
Printed and bound in Great Britain by Clays Ltd, St Ives plc

Contents

Foreword

Sorting out your pension is one of the most complicated parts of anyone's working life. Pensions are ferociously complex. There are many different types and each has its own variations.

Someone at work today with a career path that was in no way exceptional could end up with numerous sources of income in retirement, including:

- the state retirement pension;

- an additional state pension made up of a mixture of SERPS and the new S2P;

- a private pension paid for by the state in return for opting out of SERPS for some of their working life;

- one or more occupational pensions linked to jobs, with some payouts based on the salary they had when they left that job and some based on how well investments performed;

- a pension from additional savings made through an AVC scheme run by a past employer;

- a pension from stakeholder pensions, perhaps the only pension savings available in one job, which could have come with or without an employer contribution, while in another job it may have simply been a top-up in addition to an occupational pension;

- a private pension from a period of self-employment;

- savings for retirement made through ISAs and other savings schemes; and

- if these didn't add up to very much, they could well be claiming a range of means-tested benefits in addition.

It is not surprising, therefore, that polls report that few people at work today have much idea about how well off they will be when they retire. And we all know people who go for years saying that they are just about to sit down and sort out their pension, but never quite get around to it. The truth is that most people will be much worse off than they expect.

At the moment, on average, people get 60 per cent of their retirement income from the state and 40 per cent from other pension sources. Both the major political parties want to reverse these figures. While there have been some welcome moves to help the poorest pensioners, neither government nor opposition plan to increase the state retirement pension in line with earnings in future.

The TUC is one of the many groups that opposes this policy, and we continue to believe that a good state pension that goes up in line with average earnings should be the foundation for everyone's security in retirement. There is growing support for this policy as one way of cutting through some of the complexity of pensions, but when planning your pension it would probably be a little overoptimistic to bank on our campaign to overturn both Labour and Conservative policies succeeding.

We should all therefore accept that we will need an additional pension if we want to enjoy a standard of living much above the poverty line when we retire.

People with personal pensions, stakeholders and other pensions based on building up your own fund will normally buy an annuity from an insurance company when they have retired. In return for handing over some or all of your pensions pot, the company will pay a pension to you for the rest of your life. But annuity rates have fallen sharply in recent years. With people living longer, inflation falling and, at least in the last few years, stock market returns falling away, an annuity that delivers a worthwhile pension now costs much much more.

So if the state is trying to reduce its commitments and it is much tougher to build up your own pension fund, what's left?

The best kind of pension, for most people, has always been an occupational pension based on your final salary. You and your employer will both make substantial contributions while you work, and when you retire you will get a pension worked out not on the vagaries of the stock market, but based on your salary when you retire and the number of years you have worked for your employer.

I'm lucky enough to be a member of one of the post-war generations that has been well served by occupational pensions. They have rightly been called one of the great success stories of the welfare state.

For the first time a significant proportion of those retiring have had incomes above the state pension level. And indeed the combination of strong stock market performance and a desire by companies to reduce their workforces meant a lucky few were able to retire early with reasonable pensions. There is, and has been, much pensioner poverty as well, but for those lucky enough to be in jobs with good occupational pensions – both white collar and blue collar – retirement no longer means an automatic life on the breadline.

But final salary pension schemes are in decline. A number of high-profile employers have hit the headlines not just for closing their schemes to new members, but even closing them to existing members. This decline, though, had already been going on for some time before it became a news story.

The truth is that fewer of us now work for the kind of long-established large employer likely to have a good pension scheme. The public sector remains in general a good employer when it comes to pensions, but private sector employers are far more variable. Small employers and new employers are far less likely to have occupational pension schemes at all, let alone quality final salary schemes. Nearly two million fewer people are in final salary schemes today compared to the early 1990s.

The real test of whether an employer is meeting their responsibilities is not whether the scheme is a final salary scheme, but whether they are making a worthwhile contribution to any pension.

The uncomfortable conclusion is that no one today can take security in retirement for granted. We all need to take control of our pension options. Every day we put off starting a good pension will be extremely expensive when we come to retire.

This is why the TUC asked Sue Ward to write this book. Sue is one of Britain's leading pensions experts and has always been on the side of employees and pensioners trying to secure a fair deal. Best of all, she can cut through the complexities and explain pensions rules and regulations in straightforward language. That does not stop pensions being complicated, but this book does all it can to help everyone at work understand their pension arrangements.

Naturally we believe that people at work are better off in a union. The practical advice that unions can give, and their ability to take up issues with employers on behalf of a group of employees is at its most obvious when there is a pension problem.

This book is not just for trade unionists, nor does it do a hard sell for unions. When we lobby government for a better deal for pensions we do it for everyone at work. We are equally proud to have played our part in bringing this book to print and making its advice and information widely available.

John Monks, General Secretary of the TUC

Acknowledgements

I was very glad to be asked by the TUC to write this book, because it follows on from other work I have done over many years.

My first job in pensions was at the trade union then called the GMWU (now the GMB), where I learnt 'on the job' about negotiating pension schemes with employers. I used that experience to write *Pensions* in the 'Workers' Handbook' series published by Pluto Press, which came out originally in 1981. There were two later editions, re-titled the *Essential Guide to Pensions*, with additions and amendments as the pensions world changed. In the last few years, however, there have been bigger changes still, and I have long wanted to write a new book looking at the issue from the point of view of the ordinary employee.

The TUC has given me the opportunity to do this, so my thanks go to them for that, for the help and encouragement they have given me during the writing process, and for the helpful comments provided by Nigel Stanley and Michelle Lewis, their Pensions Officer. But I also want to thank employers and union representatives for all they have taught me about negotiating on pensions, and the many consultants and advisers whose brains I have picked on technical aspects over the years. My particular thanks go to the Plain English Campaign, who have allowed me to use their A–Z of Pensions in the Glossary, and the National Association of Pension Funds and Incomes Data Services, whose published material I have used extensively in different parts of the text.

Any mistakes, of course, are my own responsibility.

Sue Ward

Introduction

Most of us can expect to live well on into retirement. Some of us may spend as long a time in retirement as in work, or even longer. Those who are unfortunate enough to die early may well leave dependants – perhaps very young children – behind. Some people will also find they have to retire earlier than they might want, either because of ill health or because their jobs disappear.

The majority of people believe that state social security benefits should be adequate for us to live on in these circumstances. The fact is, however, that they are not, as Chapter 1 shows. Most people have no idea how badly off they are going to be in retirement – most of us do not really even begin thinking about our pension until we are approaching middle age.

To have a comfortable retirement, we need more resources than the state provides: savings or pension. Setting aside enough money for retirement is not easy, given all the other demands on people's wages today. The best way of ensuring that is done is if the employer sets up pension arrangements, collects and pays over contributions from the workforce, and makes a substantial employer's contribution too.

So this book is about pension arrangements set up or supported by employers:

▮ most larger employers have *occupational pension schemes* (or 'plans'). Other names are 'company' pensions or the old-fashioned term 'superannuation';

▮ there is a separate type of individualized pension, the *personal pension* (often called a 'private' pension). Anyone can set up one of these on their own, but many employers make group arrangements. These are then usually called Group Personal Pensions or GPPs;

▮ *stakeholder pensions* are a special type of personal pension. There are limits on how much you can be charged by the provider, and you cannot be penalized for transferring your pension else-where.

All except the very smallest employers must make *some* sort of pension arrangement available to the bulk of their staff. Many employers, in fact, will have all three sorts of pension arrangement running within the company at the same time for different groups of staff.

This book deals with your legal rights, what to look out for, and how to make sure the pensions are being properly looked after for all these different types of pensions. It deals with what is generally on offer to ordinary workers. It does not cover the special arrangements top managers can have, such as executive pension schemes, small self-administered pensions, or unapproved retirement benefit schemes. Nor does it deal specifically with pensions for self-employed people or those without a job. The explanations of personal and stakeholder pensions, however, will be relevant to them.

To set the scene, state pensions are covered in the next chapter.

7 *The state pension schemes*

Although this book is mainly about *non*-state pensions, most retired people would not be able to survive if they did not have state benefits to underpin them. In addition state and non-state benefits are intertwined because of the peculiar British system of 'contracting out'. So this chapter looks briefly at what you can expect:

■ when you reach state pension age;

■ if you retire early, for whatever reason;

■ if your husband or wife dies.

For more details on this very complicated topic, see the *Pensions Handbook* or the *Welfare Benefits Handbook* (details in Appendix 2).

The basic and graduated state pensions

Almost everyone gets a flat-rate basic pension, as a result of making National Insurance (NI) contributions. To receive a full basic pension, you need to have made NI contributions, or been credited with them, for nine-tenths of your working life. There are special rules to ensure that people at home looking after children or invalids, do not lose out.

In April 2002–April 2003, the basic pension is £75.50 a week. The law says that the pension must increase in line with the Retail Prices Index (RPI) each year in April. It is also possible for the government to give above-RPI increases if it wishes.

There is also a small graduated pension, for those who paid graduated NI contributions between April 1961 and April 1975. This was not properly inflation-linked, however, and as a result most pensioners who receive the graduated pension get less than £3 a week from it. During the years that it was running, there were 'contracting out' arrangements for people who belonged to their employers' pension schemes, which had to provide equivalent pension benefits (EPBs) instead.

There is also a 'non-contributory' pension for people aged 80 or more, lower than the normal basic pension (only £45.20 in 2002–03). This is payable to people who do not qualify for a basic pension, or only for part of one.

All these are taxable.

SERPS and the state second pension

Since 1978 the state has also given an earnings-related pension, commonly known as SERPS (State Earnings Related Pension Scheme), for employees (not the self-employed or those without jobs). In April 2002, SERPS was replaced by the State Second Pension (shortened to S2P). Anyone involved with pensions needs to know about SERPS as well as S2P, and a bit of the history of previous changes. There will be people who have entitlements (or contracting out arrangements) under the old arrangements for the next 40 years.

Employees who have not 'contracted out' (explained in Chapter 4) will have some SERPS if they have paid the right sort of NI contributions in any tax year since 1978–79.

Calculating SERPS

The way that SERPS is calculated is complicated, and different from the way that most non-state pension scheme benefits are worked out. Your entitlement depends on your 'band earnings' or 'reckonable earnings'. These are earnings between the lower and upper earnings limits for each tax year from 1978–79 until the year before you reach pension age. The 2001–02 limits were £72 and £575 a week, so if someone earns £300 a week, their band earnings would be (£300 – £72) = £228.

SERPS is calculated by *revaluing* these 'band earnings' for past years in line with rises in national average earnings, according to an index produced by the Department for Work and Pensions (DWP). Band earnings for each year are then added together, up to a maximum of 20 years' earnings. This figure is then divided by 80, for anyone reaching pension age before 6 April 1999. If you had contributed to SERPS for the full 20 years and reached retirement date at that point, you would receive the maximum pension of 20/80 (25 per cent) of your average revalued band earnings.

The Conservative Government changed SERPS in 1986. Originally, it had included a formula for picking out the 'best 20 years' of earnings, after they had been revalued to take account of inflation, in calculating the pension. This was abolished in 1986 without ever coming into effect, since SERPS had not run for 20 years. The maximum pension of 25 per cent was also reduced, for people reaching pension age from 6 April 1999. It is being phased down by 0.5 per cent per year from the tax year 1999–2000, and was intended to reach 20 per cent in 2009–10.

S2P takes over from 2002–03, for future years' benefits. The Government plans a two-stage reform process. In the first stage, any employee earning less than £10,800 a year but more than the lower earnings limit (explained above, currently £3,900 a year) will be treated under S2P as if their earnings were £10,800. For earnings between the lower earnings limit and £10,800 a year, the S2P will build up at double the SERPS rate: for earnings between £10,800 and £24,600, S2P will build up at half the SERPS rate; for earnings over £24,600, S2P will build up at the same rate as SERPS. So, the very low-paid are outside the system, while those who are a bit above them will do considerably better than they have done in the past under SERPS.

People can 'contract out' of S2P into a non-state pension, as they could with SERPS, with part of their NI contributions going to that other pension instead. (See Chapter 4 for an explanation of this.)

The second stage of reform is planned for 2006–07. The Government says it will only go ahead with it if stakeholder pensions are a 'success' with its target group, that is people earning between around £10,000 and £20,000 a year. It will only affect people below a certain age, probably 45, at the time it starts. They will all be treated as if they are earning only £10,800 (or the equivalent figure by then). Everyone earning more than that figure will be expected to contract out into one or other form of private pension. The Government's aim is that in the long term, 60 per cent of retirement income will come from private sources, 40 per cent from the state. Currently, the figures are the other way round.

Women and state pensions

While most men get a full state basic pension in their own right, many women do not, because of breaks in their working lives bringing up families. To help with this problem, since 1978 anyone (man or woman) who is away from work and getting Child Benefit for a dependant child (up to 16, or 19 if still in full-time education) gets 'home responsibilities protection' (HRP). There are similar rules if you are looking after a dependent invalid. This makes it easier to qualify for the basic pension under the NI rules. Most women coming up to retirement now are therefore likely to have a basic pension in their own right. If they have both their own pension and one as their husband's dependant, they get only the *higher* of the two.

Married women who are paying the old 'small stamp' (proper name 'reduced-rate National Insurance contribution') do not qualify for a state basic pension – or any other NI benefits – in their own right. They are treated just as their husbands' dependants.

HRP did not apply to the SERPS pension, but the Government has now put in some similar protection for S2P. It only applies, though, while the youngest child is under the age of 6, not right up through their schooldays as with HRP.

The age at which women can draw state pension is to be increased from 60, to match men's retirement age of 65. The change is being phased in from April 2010, with women born after 6 April 1950 the first to be affected. By 2020, any woman born after 6 March 1955 will not be able to draw a state pension until she is 65.

Means-tested benefits from the state

Many pensioners (both today and in the future) will not have enough private pension to live on, when combined with the low level of state pension. So there are also *means-tested* benefits, paid for out of taxes rather than NI contributions. To qualify, you need to show that your income and capital (that is, broadly speaking your savings and investments, but not the value of your house or personal possessions) are below a certain amount.

The Government is changing these benefits also. As these changes come into effect in October 2003, this next section covers the position both before and after that date.

Before October 2003

The main means-tested benefit is Income Support. For pensioners, within Income Support there is a Minimum Income Guarantee (MIG) set at £98.15 for a single person in 2002–03. The Government aims to increase this MIG each year broadly in line with earnings.

If you have less than your MIG entitlement, you can get extra money from the state. However, if you have more, you lose that entitlement. Pensioners on the MIG lose £1 of benefit for every £1 of other income, above that level. Anyone with capital of between £6,000 and £12,000 loses £1 from their MIG entitlement for every £250 in savings above £6,000, while anyone with capital over £12,000 cannot make a claim for MIG at all.

After October 2003

The Pension Credit is aimed at people with modest extra income or savings. Under the plans:

■ The new Pension Service will contact people shortly before they retire and ask them to claim both the basic state pension and the Credit.

■ The Guarantee Credit (a new name for the MIG) will top up a pensioner's weekly income (from basic pension, any second pension, savings and so on), up to at least £100 a week (£154 for a couple), with higher guarantees for people who are severely disabled or are carers.

■ People with higher incomes will be given an extra top-up, called the Savings Credit. For every £1 of second pension, savings or earnings above the minimum income level, 40p of the Pension Credit will be deducted. This means, for example, that someone with an occupational pension of £20 on top of the basic state pension would end up with post-Credit income £12 above the minimum income level. It has not yet been decided how to take account of earnings.

■ Pensioners will be assumed to be earning around 10 per cent interest on any capital above £6,000 (the same figure is used for a single person or a couple). There will be no top limit on the amount of capital you can have and still claim.

■ Once you have claimed at retirement, the Pension Service will recalculate the benefit each April, when the basic pension increases, without your needing to do anything. After five years, they will write to check the figures. (If your income falls during the five years, you can ask for the Pension Credit to be increased.)

■ To fit in with equal treatment rules, the Guarantee Credit will be payable to people (men or women) aged 60 or over, while the full Savings Credit will be payable to people aged 65 or over.

Many poorly-off people coming up to retirement could be better off as a result of the Pension Credit, though the worst-off will see no change as they will not have income above their basic state pension anyway. However, if you are only going to be able to build up a small occupational or personal/stakeholder pension because your earnings are low or you have started paying in late in life, it means that for every £1 of pension you build up you will only benefit by 60p. It could even be less than this, if you lose out on Housing Benefit and Council Tax Benefit as well.

State benefits if you retire early

You are not allowed to draw a state retirement pension any earlier than 65 if you are a man, 60 if you are a woman.

Jobseeker's Allowance (JSA) is the name of the benefit you can receive when you are registered as unemployed. 'Contribution-based' JSA is paid for six months, on the basis of the NI contributions you have made, taking account of any pension and earnings you have but not of the rest of your financial situation and that of your family. 'Income-based' JSA is paid on a means-tested basis (that is, taking both your capital and your income into account) for as long as you continue to qualify.

Contribution-based JSA covers the individual only, so anyone with a family needs to claim income-based JSA alongside it, as soon as they become unemployed. In working out what you are entitled to, the first £50 a week of pension from your employer, or payments from a personal pension scheme, are ignored. Above that, every penny of pension reduces JSA by the same amount. So if you had £60.50 a week of occupational pension, for instance, you would lose £10.50 a week of contribution-based JSA.

To claim income-based JSA, you must have less than £8,000 in capital. If you have more than this, you will not be able to make a claim until you have spent it down at a 'reasonable' rate.

There is also a rule that if you left your job 'voluntarily and without just cause' or because of 'misconduct' you can be disqualified from benefit for up to six months. If you chose to take early retirement of your own accord this rule would probably apply. It ought not to, however, if you have lost your job because of:

▮ compulsory redundancy; or

▮ the closure of the workplace or the firm; or

▮ you took voluntary redundancy, but the employer was looking for volunteers.

See *Changing Direction*, or the *Welfare Benefits Handbook*, for more information – details of both are in Appendix 2.

Retiring because of ill-health

If you are leaving work because of health problems, you may be eligible for Incapacity Benefit.

The NI conditions for claiming this have recently been made tougher, but anyone who has been in a steady job for some time is likely to meet them. There is then a 'personal capability test' for deciding whether you are ill enough to qualify. The aim of this is to test the extent to which your illness or disability impairs your performance of certain physical and mental functions, and whether you are capable of any sort of work. In some pilot areas, there is also an 'employability assessment' which is intended to consider what work you *can* do, if any. Some people with particular illnesses or disabilities are exempt from either test.

The *Welfare Benefits Handbook* (see Appendix 2) explains the details of the test and how it works in practice. Benefits Agency leaflets *A Guide to Incapacity Benefit* and *A Guide to the Personal Capability Assessment* give more details.

There are three basic rates of Incapacity Benefit (at 2002–03 rates):

▋ first 28 weeks of sickness (if not getting SSP): short-term lower rate (no increases for children) – £ 52.50 a week;

▋ from 29 to 52 weeks – £63.25;

▋ after one year – £70.95.

There is also an age-related allowance, paid with the long-term rate, for people who were under 45 on the first day of their present illness. There are some limited increases if you have a dependent spouse or children.

For anyone who started on Incapacity Benefit after April 2001, the benefit is reduced if you have an occupational or personal pension (or a combination) of more than £85 a week. For each £1 your pension is over this limit, your benefit is reduced by 50p. For example, if you had a pension of £100 a week (£15 over the limit), your Incapacity Benefit would be reduced by £7.50.

This rule also applies to any permanent health insurance (explained on page 111) arranged by your employer – but not to a policy that you have arranged yourself, and not if you contributed more than 50 per cent to the cost of the policy.

The effect on your early retirement decision

The best advice for anyone who has a *choice* about whether to take early retirement or not is to assume you will get nothing at all from the state until you reach state retirement age, and work out whether you will be able to live on your non-state pension and any other income or savings you might have until the state pension kicks in. If the answer is no, you probably can't afford to retire early.

If you are under 60, you may need to sign on as unemployed or sick. Even if the rules mean there is no money to come, this gives you NI credits to safeguard your state retirement pension (and will cost you nothing except a bit of hassle). Once you are over 60, you need not worry about this. A woman over 60 is above state pension age anyway (at present), while a man over 60 gets automatic NI credits, and is entitled to claim means-tested Income Support without needing to show he is looking for a job.

State benefits for widows and widowers

These changed in April 2001, with some new rights for widowers.

Almost anyone under pension age whose husband or wife dies will receive a tax-free Bereavement Payment of £2,000. After that, if you are aged 45 or over when your husband or wife dies but have not started to receive a state retirement pension, you should receive a taxable Bereavement Allowance of up to £75.50 a week for a year. For people aged between 45 and 55 when their husband or wife dies, there is a reduced 'age-related' rate. This is 7 per cent lower for each year by which you are younger than 55 (so that a 45-year-old receives only 30 per cent of the full rate). If you have dependent children when your husband or wife dies, there is a Widowed Parents' Allowance whatever your age.

Men who lost their wives before 9 April 2001, but who still met the conditions after that date, were able to start claiming Widowed Parent's Allowance from that date onwards, though it was not backdated before that date.

The Widowed Parent's Allowance is not affected by your earnings, but if you remarry you will lose it. It will also be suspended during any period when you live with someone else as husband and wife. It stops when the children are no longer dependent (which means at 16, or at 19 if still in full-time education).

Once a widow reaches 60, she can draw the state basic pension based on her deceased husband's contributions and/or her own – whichever gives her the better pension. These rules, unlike those for the new Bereavement Allowance, do still discriminate against widowers. The discrimination will only be finally ended when state retirement age is equalized from 2010. A widow will also receive half of her husband's graduated pension as well as any based on her own contributions.

Either a widow or a widower can also draw 'inherited' SERPS and S2P, as explained below, if they have received one of the widow's or bereavement allowances at any time during their lives and have not remarried since.

Inherited SERPS/S2P

As SERPS was originally designed, a widow inherited the whole of her husband's SERPS pension, so long as she was eligible for the basic widow's pension. This also applied to the widower, where both were over retirement age at the date of the wife's death.

In 1986 the Conservative Government said that if the husband's death occurred after 5 April 2000, the widow would inherit only half his SERPS pension. However, the (then) Department of Social Security ignored this change in its leaflets about the subject. As a result, many people felt they were misled and, after much pressure, the Government altered the rules. The new situation is:

▌ All men and women over state pension age on 5 October 2002 will be able to pass on 100 per cent of their SERPS entitlement, as now.

▌ For anyone within 10 years of their state retirement age in October 2002, the changes to the half rate will be phased in. It only comes fully into effect for people reaching state retirement age in October 2010 or later.

▌ A widow or widower will also be able to inherit their husband or wife's S2P. However, this will be at the 50 per cent rate from the beginning.

Benefits under the old rules

The previous rules still apply for women who lost their husbands before 9 April 2001. To summarize these briefly:

▪ If she has dependent children when her husband dies, the widow may receive a Widowed Mother's Allowance, which lasts until the youngest child is 16 (or 19 if still in full-time education).

▪ If she does not have dependent children, but is between 55 and 64, she may receive a widow's pension, followed by a state retirement pension.

▪ If she is aged over 55 when the Widowed Mother's Allowance runs out, she moves on to the widow's pension at that point.

▪ If she is between 45 and 55 when either of these things happens, she receives a reduced 'age-related' widow's benefit.

Widowers were discriminated against under the old rules but, as explained above, those with dependent children can start drawing the new Widowed Parent's Allowance from 9 April 2001, whenever it was they lost their partner.

2 The different types of pension scheme

This chapter starts off by explaining the broad principles of pensions and then goes into some of the main variations. The small print of pension scheme design – which can make all the difference between a good scheme and a bad one – is covered in later chapters.

Whatever the design of the scheme, what matters in the end is how much money is going into it, from contributions and investment returns. You can't get a quart out of a pint pot. However fancy the scheme design, if there is not much money there, there won't be much of a pension.

Salary-related pensions

The name describes how your pension is calculated – it is linked to your salary, or pay, by a particular mathematical formula. The other term for these schemes is 'defined benefit', because the rules of the scheme lay down what *benefit* you are entitled to when you retire or leave.

Final-salary schemes

These are the most usual types of salary-related scheme. To work out your pension, you need to know first how your scheme rules define four things:

- pensionable salary;

- *final* pensionable salary;

- pensionable service; and

- the 'accrual rate' (the rate at which the pension builds up each year).

Your pension scheme booklet should include definitions of the first three, usually in a list at the front or the back. Different schemes use different names for the same thing, so the first item for example might be 'scheme salary', 'pensionable earnings', 'pensionable pay' or any one of many other names, but if you read through the list of definitions it ought to be clear. The last item, the accrual rate, may be included in the definitions or you may have to look at the explanation in the booklet of how the pension is worked out. It will usually be a fraction (such as 1/60th) or a percentage (such as 1.5 per cent).

Having got these figures, the formula is that to work out the pension, one must take the final pensionable salary figure, multiply it by the 'accrual rate' (the fraction, or percentage, which builds up each year), and multiply it by the length of pensionable employment (often called 'pensionable service') the person has had.

In the simplest scheme, pensionable salary is the same as your gross salary, and final pensionable salary would be your pensionable salary in the last 12 months before you retire. The most common accrual rate is 1/60th, and most schemes say that pensionable service is simply the years and complete months you have worked for that employer since you joined the scheme.

Dave joined the ABC company scheme at 25, and is now due to retire at 65, so he has exactly 40 years' pensionable service. His gross pay, in the last year before he retires, is £24,000 a year. So £24,000 x 1/60 (which is the same as dividing by 60) = £400; £400 x 40 = £16,000.

Career-average salary schemes

These are also salary-related, but in this case they take your pensionable salary for each year you have been in the scheme, and average it out to give a final figure. Because of inflation, the earnings figures in the past now look very low compared to today's figures, so before doing this averaging the figures are usually *revalued* to take account of the way earnings have risen generally in the meantime, or possibly only in line with the way prices have risen.

Dave's twin sister Davina is in one of these schemes. To calculate her pension, the scheme's computer takes the figures for her annual earnings for the last 40 years, and uprates them in line with National Average Earnings (NAE) in that time. Davina's pay has generally been lower than Dave's, but it is now the same because she was promoted two years ago. Averaging her earnings involves adding together all the recalculated figures and dividing by 40, which gives Davina a figure of £22,000. From then on, the pension is worked out in the same way as for Dave's. She will end up with £15,333 a year.

These schemes are rare, but the supermarket chain Tesco introduced one in 2001, with guaranteed revaluation limited only to prices. The argument is that it is fairer to take account of your overall working pattern through your working life, rather than just the pay you happen to be given in the last few years.

Integrated pension schemes

An *integrated* pension scheme (also called 'clawback') is one where a certain amount is deducted to take account of the state pension. It can be a deduction from pensionable pay, from the pension itself, or both.

One form of integration is for the pensionable salary to be calculated minus a figure related either to the state basic pension or the Lower Earnings Limit (LEL), which is used in calculating the SERPS pension. The two figures are generally within £1 of each other. The deduction might be 1.5 times the LEL, the same, or 0.5 times the LEL. Alternatively, it could be a fixed money figure, perhaps based on what the pension was a few years ago.

Jim Smith has final earnings of £15,000 a year. But his pension scheme is integrated, so an amount equal to the Lower Earnings Limit is deducted before his pensionable earnings are calculated. The LEL is £3,900 as a yearly figure, and £15,000 minus £3,900 is £11,100.

Jim has been in the scheme 10 years, and it is a 1/60th scheme. So 10/60ths of £11,100 is £1,850.

Alternatively, the scheme can build the integration into the pension, so that for each year someone has been in the employer's scheme, a fraction of the state pension is deducted. So first you work out the pension, and then you must find the appropriate slice of the state pension to be deducted, before you get the final result.

> Mary Jones' scheme gives a pension of 1/60th of full earnings, minus 1/40th of the LEL, for every year she is in the scheme. Her final pensionable earnings are £15,000 and the LEL is £3,900 a year. She also has 10 years of service. So her pension for each year of service is (£15,000 divided by 60) = £250, minus (£3,900 divided by 40 = £97.50) = £152.50 per year, or £1,525 after 10 years.

Money-purchase pensions

Again, the name explains these: the pension you get depends on how much money has been put away for you by the time you retire, and what it will buy then. Another name for these schemes is 'defined contribution' because the promise from the employer is only that they will *put in* a certain amount.

In the simplest type, the way this works is:

▪ each year, the employer and employee both put in a fixed percentage of earnings, for example 5 per cent;

▪ this money is then invested in a fund until retirement, with the investment returns building up each year;

▪ when the member reaches retirement, she or he will have built up a fund of all the contributions that have gone in, and all the investment returns that have been added;

▪ this fund is then passed over to an insurance company, which in return provides an 'annuity' – that is, a pension – each year for as long as the person lives.

So this is much like any other savings scheme, except that you get special tax advantages and have to use the money to give you an income after you retire, rather than being able to spend it as you like. In most money-purchase schemes, you can in fact have some of the money as a lump sum, and you can postpone buying the annuity and draw your income direct from the fund, called 'income drawdown', as explained later.

Teodor is putting 5 per cent and his employer is putting 10 per cent of his wages into a money-purchase pension scheme for him. By the time he comes to retire after 40 years, around £40,000 has gone in altogether in contributions, and it has earned another £160,000 in investment returns, making a total of £200,000. For every £10,000 that's in the fund, Teodor can buy an annuity of around £800 a year, so 20 x £800 gives him a pension of £16,000.

Teodor has ended up with the same pension as Dave in our previous example, but the difference between his money-purchase scheme and Dave's final-salary one is that the money-purchase pension is much more variable. When Teodor checked what was in his pension fund in 2000, it was bigger than it is now because the shares it was invested in were doing very well at the time. Since then, their prices have fallen. The insurance companies have also discovered from the statistics that men retiring now can expect to live longer than men who retired a few years ago, so they have reduced the amount of annuity they will give for each £10,000 of cash.

There are ways of reducing the chances of the pension going down (or up) as you come close to retirement. The main one is called 'lifestyling' and is explained in Chapter 9.

Hybrids

These follow a mixture of the two principles. One version is the *money-purchase underpin* in a final-salary scheme. The pension is calculated on a final-salary basis, but if your contributions and possibly also part of those the employer has made, along with the investment returns that the fund has made, can buy you a bigger pension, then you get that instead. Usually this means that people who are retiring will have a pension that links to their earnings, while younger people who are leaving rather than retiring get a pension on the money-purchase basis to take elsewhere.

Some schemes work the other way round, with the pension generally being money-purchase, but a promise that it can't fall below (say) 1/80th of your earnings for each year of service, however badly the investments are doing.

In a *targeted defined contribution* scheme the money is invested on a money-purchase basis, but a close eye is kept on what the fund is going to produce as a pension and, if there is likely to be a shortfall, more money is put in. These are fairly common among senior managers and directors of small companies, but really only count as a hybrid if there is a formal binding arrangement to top-up the fund if necessary. If it is just a vague 'we'll see you all right' it may not be very valuable.

Hybrids share the investment risk between the employee and the employer. Who takes the bigger share, however, depends on just how the scheme is designed. The best give the employees 'the best of both worlds'. In the less good ones, the member may have an illusion of security without actually gaining anything.

If you have a peculiar design of scheme, it is important to under-stand what is being offered. Employers will invent their own names for these and the same name can be used for very differ-ent packages.

For example, drug manufacturer Astra Zeneca has what it describes as a 'cost balance plan'. It works as a money-purchase scheme for younger workers, but at 45 everyone has the right to transfer over to a 'retirement account', which is a final-salary scheme with the benefits expressed as 'credits' in a retirement account. It is a good, if complicated, scheme.

The same name, though, is used for a US version where the employer and/or employee pays in a percentage of pay each year to the individual's account. This is then guaranteed to be increased each year at a *notional* rate (this is the important bit), which can be quite low. The actual contributions are invested by the trustees (explained in Chapter 6), who are probably able to get a better return. According to one report, 10 million employ-ees in the US have these and 45 per cent of the employers have reduced their pension costs as a result.[1]

Flexible benefits plans

Flexible benefit or 'flex' plans are not a particular type of benefit, but a way of linking together the different non-wage benefits avail-able for the employee.

The idea is that all the various benefits – such as cars, health care, holidays, pensions and life insurance – are given a unit value and each person can choose their own package of benefits. So, for example, you could swap a company car for extra life insurance.

Pensions are not always included in a flex scheme, and it is simpler to include them when it is a money-purchase rather than a final-salary scheme. Often there will be a 'core' level of benefits you cannot give up (perhaps 1/80ths with two times earnings death benefit), but you can then decide for yourself if you want to add extra pension or death benefit up to the IR limits (explained in Appendix 1).

Legal frameworks for pension schemes

As well as the question of the way the pension builds up, there is the question of the type of legal arrangement under which the scheme has been set up. The two main types are occupational and personal.

A stakeholder pension is a special variety of personal pension. (In theory it is possible to have a stakeholder pension that is a special variety of occupational scheme, but there are very few, so we will ignore those rules.)

All *salary-related* schemes (of whichever variety) and most *hybrid* schemes (that is, except some of the *targeted defined contribution* ones) must be occupational pension schemes. This is because the employer is standing behind the promise to bail it out if things go wrong. It is only with money-purchase pensions that the choice between occupational and personal to start with, and then ordinary personal and stakeholder, arises.

Occupational schemes

An occupational scheme is set up by an employer, or by groups of employers to cover a whole industry; the Universities Superannuation Scheme (USS), for example, is open to staff in all the universities in the UK. The employers make the rules and – with some safeguards for the members – can change them.

Occupational schemes can be salary-related, money-purchase, or hybrid. In the public services, such as the Civil Service and the health service, the pension arrangements are set up under Acts of Parliament, and ultimately looked after by the Treasury. Local government employees also have a scheme set up by Act of Parliament, but in this case it is specific local councils who look after the pensions. These are all called *statutory* schemes.

Outside these areas, occupational schemes are set up under a *trust*, and there are *trustees* who are looking after the funds. Generally, these will be a mixture of senior management and people nominated by the scheme members, as explained in Chapter 6. Especially in a smaller company, the trustees may have handed over all the work of running the scheme to an insurance company or a firm of financial advisers. Alternatively, the administration work may have been 'outsourced' to another company that specializes in it. The Teachers' Scheme, for instance, has a firm called Capita doing all the administration. It's also usual for an insurance company, a bank, or another financial institution to be managing the investments.

You must have an employment connection with the particular employer or group of employers, to be a member of that occupational scheme. So for example university lecturers can move between different universities and stay with the USS, but if they decide to go and work in the private sector, they must leave the USS (though they can still leave the pension they have built up with the scheme).

To be approved by the Inland Revenue as an occupational scheme, the employer as well as the employee has to be putting in contributions – though these can be very small – and the trustees have to stick to the rules about maximum benefits, explained in Appendix 1. You pay contributions to an occupational scheme out of your gross pay, and so get tax relief immediately, through having a lower figure for the income from which tax is deducted.

Personal pension schemes

Personal pension (PP) schemes are *always* money-purchase. Your rights in a PP depend on the individual contract between each member and the personal pension 'provider'. Most of these providers are insurance companies, plus some banks and other big financial institutions. The details of your contract are included in the 'policy document' that you should be given when you sign up.

Some employers have set up 'group personal pensions' (GPPs) and may have put their names and logos on the pension literature. These are still individual PPs, though. The employer is simply arranging for the employees to be able to buy a particular package – normally with lower charges than if each individual were going out and buying it separately – and hopefully will also be making a contribution.

If you leave your employer, you are allowed to carry on paying into a PP. But any employer's contribution will stop, and so may any special scale of charges.

The Inland Revenue has rules about the structure of benefits in a PP, but not about the amount that can be paid out as a pension. Instead, it lays down the maximum contributions that can be paid *in*, as contributions each year. You pay your contributions to a PP scheme out of your net (take-home) pay, and the provider then claims basic-rate tax back from the Inland Revenue.

Since April 2001, it's been possible for an occupational money-purchase scheme to be set up (or converted) so that it follows the Inland Revenue rules for personal pensions. There are some advantages but rather more disadvantages in doing so, and it doesn't seem likely there will ever be very many of these.

Stakeholder pensions

As explained above, these are a special type of personal pension. For some stakeholder schemes, like the one the TUC runs, there are trustees looking after the scheme, but individuals still build up rights under their individual contracts with the provider. Stakeholder schemes come under strict limits on how much the provider can charge, and there must be no extra charges when you start or stop paying, or move your money somewhere else. There are also rules about employer access – the employer offering you the chance to join a stakeholder scheme and contributing through payroll.

Note

1. _New Global Investors_, pp 97–99, quoting _Business Week_, 24 April 2000, online edition.

3 *The rules for pensions provided by employers*

There are a large number of rules about the way pension schemes are set up and run. Many of these come from the Inland Revenue (IR), which is interested because both you and the employer get tax relief on pension contributions (worth nearly £13 billion a year). Others come from the government and the European Union, which are interested in having fairness between different groups of employees, and also in ensuring that promises made by employers or commercial providers are worth something.

As the IR's rules on the maximum benefits and contributions you can have are very technical, we have put them in Appendix 1. This chapter deals with:

▌ the rules banning discrimination against various groups;

▌ voluntary membership of pension schemes;

▌ the rules about when an employer must provide access to the different sorts of scheme;

▌ the rules about payment of contributions, especially those that employers collect from employees to pass over to the pension scheme or provider;

▌ pensions and divorce.

Rules about discrimination

Equal treatment between men and women

Up until 1975, the rules of pension schemes often said that women could not join at all, or had to wait longer than a man. Rules like this had to be changed in 1975, but there could still be rules that – while they did not specifically say that they kept women out – had the same effect. The greatest example of this, by far, was for part-time workers, most of whom are women. If only full-time workers could join the scheme, in the average workplace far more women than men would be affected. So this was *indirect* discrimination.

Schemes could also still pay different benefits to men and women, or to their dependants when they died. Often here it was men rather than women who lost out, because schemes provided widows' pensions but not widowers' pensions.

This position changed thanks to the European Union. In 1990, in the *Barber* case, the European Court decided that pensions ought to be considered as deferred pay for the purposes of the Treaty of Rome (as it then was). Since Article 119 of this said that there must be equal pay for men and women, it had to apply to pensions as well. They left it vague, though, whether people could claim arrears for back service, or only for the future, which meant further court cases to clarify it.

The Pensions Act 1995 laid down that there must be equal treatment between men and women. The Act writes in a rule in every pension scheme, even if there isn't one there already. The rule covers the qualifications for scheme membership, the treatment of members and their dependants, and related discretionary powers, including the way in which they are exercised.

There are some big exceptions to the rule, however, related to the fact that, on average, women live longer than men and so are more expensive to provide a pension for. So, for example, schemes that reduce the pension if you take early retirement (explained on page 80) can reduce it by different amounts for women and men of the same age.

Schemes are not allowed to discriminate between men and women in the amount of lump sum death benefit they pay, but they can offer different amounts depending on whether a widow/er's pension is paid or not.

Money-purchase schemes are also allowed to buy women different annuities from men at the same age, for the same amount of money in their pension account. Where a scheme is contracted out, however (explained in Chapter 4), for the part of the pension that replaces SERPS/S2P the annuity must be 'unisex', that is, equal between men and women.

Claims for past service are still a thorny subject. The 1995 Pensions Act laid down the same time limits for making claims as for equal pay – six months after the end of the discrimination complained of. For this purpose, the 'end' of the discrimination is when the person leaves the job. It also said that any arrears could be backdated for two years at most, which meant that people who had been kept out of their pension schemes for years, and were perhaps now quite close to retirement, could gain very little.

The unions, coordinated by the TUC, fought strongly to have these limits overturned, and finally did so at the beginning of 2001. They set up a series of test cases, called the *Preston* cases, which went all the way to the European Court and back to the House of Lords. The European judges decided that the two-year limit was unfair, and so people can claim backdated pension rights as far back as 1976.

The judges said that the six-month time limit for making a claim after leaving that employment was valid. However, where there had been a series of short-term contracts with one employer and a 'stable employment relationship', this six months should only start to run after the end of the last contract. This was particularly good news for teachers and school staff who had been on term-time only contracts.

No one knows the total bill, or how many women have benefited. There are 60,000 women who had to put in formal claims to employment tribunals, and these have been slowly worked through since the final court decision. The better employers, especially in the financial sector which is a large employer of part-time workers, decided to offer credits in the pension scheme without waiting for the court decision.

> *Note.* If you are a part-time worker who was kept out of your pension scheme in the past, *and* are still working for the same employer, you could still have a claim for backdated service in the pension scheme. Otherwise, you would need to have made a claim within six months. Look at *Your Rights at Work* (see Appendix 2) for how to make a claim. You could also ask your union for advice if you are a member, or a law centre or Citizens Advice Bureau (CAB) if not. The Equal Opportunities Commission (EOC, address in Appendix 4) may also be able to assist. Employment Tribunal claim forms and other information are available from their helpline (08457 959775).

Part-time workers now

Since July 2000, the Part-time Workers (Prevention of Less Favourable Treatment) Regulations have been in force. As you might expect from the title, these say that part-time employees must not be treated less favourably than full-time staff. So where full-time staff are eligible for a pension scheme, part-timers in the same category must be also, unless there is 'objective justification' for different treatment. The benefits from the pension scheme for part-time staff should be on a pro-rata basis – that is, proportionate to what full-time staff get.

For example, someone in the Local Government pension scheme, working half the normal hours, would have his or her pension based on a full-time equivalent salary, but each year's service would be counted as six months.

You need to have a full-time 'comparator', so if everyone is part-time it does not really help. However, the existing European law explained above is still in force and can be used as a fallback.

Retirement ages

The Sex Discrimination Act 1987 says that women must not be made to retire earlier than men in the same category of employment. This affects retirement from employment, but not from the pension scheme.

Occupational schemes have needed to have equal retirement ages for men and women since the *Barber* judgment in 1990, if they are not to fall foul of European law. The position is complicated, but essentially:

■ if a scheme had unequal retirement ages before 17 May 1990, these can still be used in the calculation of pension built up before that date;

■ if a scheme took a while to equalize after that date, the disadvantaged group can make a claim to be brought up to the level of the advantaged group;

■ when a scheme does equalize, it can do so by worsening one group's position, rather than improving the other's.

So in many schemes, the different 'slices' of pension are calculated on the basis of different retirement ages. Typically, the scheme might say that:

■ for service up to 17 May 1990, pension is calculated on the basis of 60 for women, 65 for men;

■ for service between 17 May 1990 and (say) 6 April 1994 – the date the rules changed – it is calculated as if both sexes retire at 60;

■ for service since the date the rules changed, it is calculated as if both sexes retire at 65.

This therefore gives a slight gain to the men but a loss to the women, because they have lost the chance to go at 60. Although this is acceptable in terms of European law, there are doubts about whether employers have got things right in the way they made the change, under UK employment law. This is because the age at which you retire is usually part of your contractual terms, and an employer cannot make a fundamental change to your contract to your detriment, without your consent. (See *Your Rights at Work*, details in Appendix 2, for more information on this.) It is not clear legally, however, how far a change in retirement age is 'fundamental'. It probably is, if you were in your late 50s when the change was made. It probably is not, if you were in your 20s. There have not so far been any legal cases on this point, however.

This means that if the employer simply announced the change without asking for people's consent, or made the change even when people protested, it might not be valid. So when women in this situation reach 60, they may be able to claim their right to retire. If they succeed, their male colleagues will also then be able to claim equality with them!

Equal treatment and personal/stakeholder pensions

The rules explained above cover 'employer-provided benefits' generally. So if the employer is putting a contribution into a personal or stakeholder scheme for some people but not for others, the equal treatment rules would certainly cover them. If they are only passing on a deduction from pay to a stakeholder scheme, they might try to argue that this was not an employer-provided benefit, but they would then be breaking other rules about 'employer access' so this would not do them much good. There have not been any test cases on it, however.

On the other hand, if you shopped around for your own pension, and are paying into it through a direct debit, the employer would not be involved. You might have a case against an insurance company or financial adviser, though. Ask the Equal Opportunities Commission (address in Appendix 4) for advice.

Temporary workers

In the past, it has been very common for employers to say that the pension scheme applies only to permanent workers, and then to pick and choose who is counted as 'permanent'. This is due to change, though all the details were not clear at the time of writing, because of a new European Directive on Fixed-term Work.

The aim, broadly, is to prevent this group of workers from being discriminated against. A fixed-term worker, for these purposes, is anyone on an employment contract the end of which is determined by 'objective conditions' – that is, on a contract ending when a specified date is reached, a specified task is completed or a specified event happens.

The draft Fixed-term Employees (Prevention of Less Favourable Treatment) Regulations 2001, say that fixed-term workers should not be less favourably treated than similar permanent employees in their contractual terms and conditions of employment unless there is an 'objective reason' to justify it. The Government had been trying to avoid including pay and pensions, but seems to have concluded it cannot do so.

To be able to make a claim under the Regulations, you will need to be able to point to a comparator on an indefinite contract. You can, though, look outside the immediate place of work to someone else working for the same employer.

To enforce these requirements, individuals would have to take the employer, or the pension scheme, to an Employment Tribunal. It would be sensible to raise it with the employer and the trustees first, to see if a change can be negotiated which will cover a wider group.

Maternity and family leave

Since 1973, schemes have had to re-admit employees returning from maternity leave, and periods of pensionable service must be added together to count as continuous pensionable service. On top of this, all pregnant employees are entitled to a minimum of 18 weeks' maternity leave. During this, all the terms and conditions of an employee's contract have to be preserved with the exception of 'monetary remuneration', that is, the pay packet itself, and all employees must be able to accrue pension rights during any paid maternity leave to which they are contractually or statutorily entitled.

These rules mean that, in a final-salary scheme:

▌ the member must continue to build up pensionable service;

▌ she need only pay employee contributions calculated on the actual maternity pay she is receiving; but

▌ the employer must continue to pay any earmarked contributions calculated on the basis of her normal pay; and

■ preserved pension or transfer values calculated after the start of maternity leave (if, for instance, she decides to give in her notice while she is away) must be based on the pay she would have received had she been working normally (these are explained in Chapter 5);

■ death in service benefits must be maintained.

In money-purchase schemes, the position is the same except that, if the employee only pays contributions based on her actual maternity pay, the amount of her pension will be reduced. Some lawyers suggest that the employer needs to top up her contributions to compensate for the shortfall, but this has not been tested in a legal case.

There are also rules about family leave, which means 'any period throughout which a member is absent from work for family reasons'. There is a right to up to 13 weeks' unpaid family leave, for employees with more than one year's service and children under 5.

In general, when someone returns to work after parental leave it must be on terms and conditions that are no less favourable than if he or she had not been absent. The periods of pensionable service before and after the leave must be treated as continuous. For any period of paid parental or family leave, pension should continue to accrue, but only on the basis of the amounts actually paid.

Personal/stakeholder schemes

You can retain your membership of these, and continue to pay into them, whether you are earning or not (see Chapter 9 for more details). If the employer is making a contribution to the scheme, this should be continued during paid maternity or family leave, and you ought still to be covered by any life assurance arranged by the employer.

People with disabilities

The Disability Discrimination Act 1995 gives people with disabilities some protection against being discriminated against in the pension scheme. Keeping someone out of a pension scheme because of a particular medical condition, for instance, would be discrimination unless the trustees of the scheme could justify their action, for example, by pointing to a *substantial* extra risk that the employee would have to take early retirement due to ill heath.

It is, though, possible for the person to be excluded from some benefits (like ill health retirement) but charged the same contribution as anyone else. But schemes cannot do it the other way round and charge more for the same benefits. You cannot ask for the equivalent of the employer's contribution to be paid as wages if you are excluded from the scheme.

Any exclusion, or separate package of benefits, can only be created at the beginning of the person's membership. So the trustees cannot suddenly say a few years later, 'Well, now you've got a heart condition, we are excluding you from the benefits that might be most valuable to you.'

Insurance companies providing a benefit package for an employer are also covered by the Act.

See the Disability Rights Commission booklet *The Disability Discrimination Act 1995: What employees and job applicants need to know* (DLE3), or look on the Web site, www.drc-gb.org for more information. If you run into problems, contact your union, a law centre or CAB, or the DRC (address in Appendix 4).

Other forms of discrimination

Discussions are also going on about widening rules on discrimination to cover age, sexual orientation or religious belief. This is because of another European Directive, the Employment Framework Directive, due to be implemented in 2006.

Voluntary membership of pension schemes

By law, it must be voluntary for employees to join or not to join their pension scheme, and members must be allowed to leave at any time. There are, however, ways of increasing the chances that people will join, without breaking the law:

▌ scheme rules can say 'you are automatically assumed to want to join, unless you opt out';

▌ schemes can sign people up to the pension scheme as soon as they join the employer, even if there is a waiting period before they actually start building up pension rights (so long as the position is fully explained); and

▌ anyone who does not want to join, or who wants to leave, can be asked to have an interview with someone who can explain what they are losing, and/or fill in a form to say they understand what they are giving up, and take it home to their spouse or partner to fill in as well.

It's also legal to say that if someone does not join at the first opportunity, he or she has lost the chance and cannot join in the future.

If there is a pension scheme that you are entitled to join, you have a right to be told the details of it (see Chapter 11).

'Access' to a stakeholder pension

Since October 2001, employers have had to provide 'access' to a stakeholder scheme for people for whom they do not provide another sort of pension. This means that the employer must:

I 'designate' a registered stakeholder scheme;

I provide information to the relevant employees; and

I allow representatives of the scheme reasonable access to them.

Before making the final selection, or before changing stakeholder schemes, the employer must 'consult' the relevant employees and their organizations.

Many employers with good schemes do not need to designate at all, because they can claim exemption or have no relevant employees.

Exemptions

Small employers, of fewer than five people, are exempt. For this purpose, any employee is counted, no matter how short the hours on their contract, or what their earnings level is. If a fifth person is taken on, there is a further three months' grace for the employer to make the necessary arrangements.

Anyone who has earned below the Lower Earnings Limit (£75 a week in 2002–03) in any week in the last three months need not be offered access. (These employees do count, however, so far as the 'fewer than five' exemption is concerned.)

Any employer who runs an occupational pension scheme is exempt from offering stakeholder access to anyone who has joined the scheme, and to anyone who is eligible but has decided *not* to join. For this purpose, an 'occupational scheme' can just provide lump sum death benefit and no pension.

The employer must then offer access to all other 'relevant employees'; that is, all those who do not fit into the previous categories, except those who:

■ will qualify to join the pension scheme within the next 12 months;

■ would be able to join if they were over 18, or were not within five years of the scheme's normal pension age;

■ have been employed for less than three months; or

■ are not eligible for the pension scheme because of IR rules (as controlling directors, for instance).

Alternatively, an employer who has a GPP scheme for all the relevant employees, is making a contribution of at least 3 per cent of basic pay towards that scheme, and is willing to deduct from pay and pass on contributions if employees wish, can claim exemption. The employer can ask employees to match their contribution, but only up to the 3 per cent level. If the scheme was established before 8 October 2001, the 'matching' requirement can go up to 5 per cent. For any future GPP arrangement, it must be a term of employees' contracts that the employer will make the 3 per cent (or more) contribution. For those already in place in October 2001, however, it is enough if the arrangement has been treated as contractual.

The GPP must impose no additional charges or penalties for exit or for stopping contributions, though this has been rather loosely defined.

Note. You can find out if your employer should be providing access to a stakeholder pension for you by looking at the decision trees on the OPAS Web site for stakeholders (www.stakeholder-helpline.org.uk). There is a similar one from the employer's point of view at www.opra.gov.uk.

If the employer does not provide access to a stakeholder scheme when they should, the employees (or their union) can complain to Opra (explained on page 160). They will then investigate and have the power to fine an employer up to £50,000.

You do not have to join the scheme your employer has chosen, but can join another one instead. The employer, however, only has to offer payroll deductions for the 'designated' scheme. Not many employers seem to be making contributions towards their employees' stakeholder schemes, but if they do, they are allowed to say that they will do so only for their designated scheme. However, if the employer changes the designated scheme, people who want to carry on their payroll deductions to the old scheme must be allowed to do so.

Rules about when contributions must be paid in

There are strict rules about when the employees' and employers' contributions must be passed over to any sort of pension arrangement. The employer can be fined for not keeping to them, and being 'knowingly concerned in the fraudulent evasion' of payment is a criminal offence.

All types of scheme need to have a written record of what is due to be paid over. The name of this, and what it must contain, varies between the different sorts:

▌ for a final-salary scheme, it is a 'schedule of contributions', and needs to be agreed between employer and trustees every three years after the actuarial valuation (see the Glossary, Appendix 5);

▌ for a money-purchase occupational scheme, a 'schedule of payments' must be drawn up annually between the employer and trustees;

▌ for a personal/stakeholder scheme, it is a 'record of payments due', showing the due dates for contributions (both employer's and employee's separately) and the rate of contribution.

If a pension contribution is deducted from an employee's pay in one month, it must be paid across by the 19th of the following month at the latest, whether it is an occupational scheme or a personal/stakeholder scheme. For example, contributions deducted in April must be paid over by 19 May.

The *employer's* contribution must be paid over on or before the date shown on the schedule or record. This date can be different from that for the employees' contributions, but it is generally more convenient if they are the same.

The pension scheme trustees or the provider should monitor the contributions coming in, and report to Opra if they are late. If they do not, then at least for an occupational scheme the shortfall is likely to be picked up by the auditor at the end of the year, and he or she will report to Opra instead.

Pensions and divorce

There have been two recent legal changes that have made it possible – though very complex – to divide a pension when a couple divorces.

The first is 'earmarking'. This means that once the pension starts being paid, it is divided between the member and the ex-spouse according to a judge's order. It dies with the member, and if the ex-spouse remarries he or she loses it.

Very few earmarking orders have been made. A new system of 'pension-sharing' was introduced in December 2000. This means that:

■ your solicitor asks you to obtain details of the transfer value (explained in Chapter 5) from the pension scheme;

■ the court may order that part of this is passed over to the other spouse;

■ the amount that has been passed over to the other spouse is treated as a 'debit' from the original pension. If he or she earns less than a quarter of the earnings cap (explained on page 162) the member can put in extra contributions to build what's left back up to the maximum the IR allows. If he or she earns more than this, however, the 'debit' has to be treated as if it is still part of the pension, when calculating what the maximum is.

Where both spouses are young, or both have roughly equal pensions the courts will probably not make any pension order. It is where one person has much greater pension expectations than the other – a firefighter whose wife has been working part time while looking after young children, for instance – that it will apply. Even then, other assets, such as the value of an owner-occupied house or a share portfolio, will probably be divided instead where this is possible, as it is simpler and clearer.

Personal pensions and stakeholder pensions can also be divided. For these, it will mean dividing the money in the fund so that each partner can have their own 'pot' and build up a pension on their own account.

Finding out more

Your pension scheme's trustees should have taken a decision on whether they will keep the ex-spouse's pension credit in the fund, or insist on it being transferred elsewhere. Most public sector schemes do the former, most private sector schemes the latter.

They should also have decided what they will charge for providing the figures and doing the necessary work. The pension scheme should have made an announcement about this, at the end of 2000 or the beginning of 2001. If not, ask the scheme administrator for information.

If you are living with someone but not married to him or her, then the pension cannot be divided if you split up.

4 Contracting out of SERPS and S2P

What 'contracting out' means

Contracting out means that, while you still get your *basic* state pension, you give up your rights to the second state pension (formerly SERPS and now S2P). Instead, you are paid a pension from your employer or from a personal/stakeholder scheme. In return for what you give up, depending on what sort of pension arrangement you are in, you get either a reduction in your National Insurance (NI) contributions, or part of your NI contributions, having been collected from you, paid across to the people providing the pension.

Contracting out started in 1978, and there have been several changes and additions to the system since then. This makes it exceedingly complicated. This chapter deals with the way contracting out works for people who are current members of one or other variety of pension scheme. Chapter 5 explains what happens when you leave the scheme.

In many cases the pension arrangement is contracted *in*. This means that you pay your full NI contributions, plus whatever contributions you need to make to the pension scheme, and when you retire you receive both SERPS/S2P and the other pension, in full. The Inland Revenue does not count SERPS/S2P against its maximum limits (explained in Appendix 1) so you can build up more in total pension that way. The drawback is that it will cost you or the employer, or both, more money as you will be making double contributions.

There are some very good reasons for being contracted in, especially for older people in money-purchase occupational schemes or personal/stakeholder schemes. If a new pension arrangement is being discussed, or the existing one renegotiated, it is worth asking whether the issue has been fully reviewed.

The different forms of contracting out

There are three different forms of contracting out:

▮ 'contracted out salary-related' (COSR) schemes, which used to provide a Guaranteed Minimum Pension (GMP) but now have to have benefits at least as good as a 'reference scheme';

▮ 'contracted out money-purchase' (COMP) schemes, which have to have a minimum contribution going in, and receive an 'age-related rebate' from the state; and

▮ 'appropriate personal pensions' (APPs) which also have an age-related rebate paid from the state. These included contracted out stakeholder pensions.

COSR schemes

Final-salary schemes are generally 'contracted out salary-related' (COSR). This means that the scheme benefits have to be checked against a 'reference scheme' set out in the Pensions Act 1995. The scheme's actuary must certify whether or not the scheme meets this standard, for 90 per cent or more of the scheme members, and to re-certify this every three years. There is no guarantee, for any member, that their pension will be as good as, or better than, SERPS or S2P.

The 'reference scheme' has a retirement age of 65 and:

▮ 'qualifying earnings' are 90 per cent of the employee's earnings between the lower and upper earnings limits (explained on page 4);

▮ the pension builds up at 1/80th of final qualifying earnings (averaged over the last three years) per year of service; and

▮ widows' and widowers' pensions are half the members' pensions, calculated at the date they died. It is allowable for these to be paid for out of the lump sum death benefit, though few schemes do this.

The scheme only has to provide 'broadly equivalent' benefits, so for instance a scheme where only basic earnings were pensionable, but where the pension built up at 1/60th per year of service, would qualify.

Before April 1997: GMPs

The rules explained above have only existed since April 1997. Before then, COSR schemes had to provide a 'guaranteed minimum pension' (GMP), calculated to be equivalent to your SERPS entitlement. (The two sets of rules were not quite the same, but the state made up any shortfall.) The scheme had to guarantee that at the state retirement age of 65 for men, 60 for women, the GMP would be payable. There also had to be a widows' or widowers' GMP (explained below). When the new rules came in, GMPs built up before April 1997 were safeguarded. So they will continue to be paid for the next 40 years or so.

You are not allowed to 'commute' any of your GMP for cash. (See Chapter 8 for an explanation of this.) Particularly for people taking early retirement, this can mean that you get much less as a lump sum than the IR would allow (explained in Appendix 1) or even none at all. The only exception is that if the pension is *trivial*, which means under £260 a year, you will be allowed to take it all.

Pension increases

Again, what a contracted out scheme has to provide has changed over the years, with changes in government pension policy. Originally, when contracting out started in 1978, the state picked up the bill for keeping the GMP (but not the rest of the pension) in line with rises in the RPI. In 1988 the law changed to say that the first 3 per cent of any increase in the GMP had to come from the scheme, with the state picking up the rest. When GMPs were abolished for future service under the Pensions Act, final earnings schemes were told to increase the whole pension accrued after April 1997, by 5 per cent or the rise in the RPI, whichever was the lower. This is called Limited Pension Indexation (LPI) and applies to both contracted in and contracted out schemes. Except if the person has retired due to ill health, the increases need not be given to someone who has retired aged less than 55, but a 'catch-up' exercise needs then to be done at 55.

Spouses' pensions

For the pension that built up between 1978 and 1988, a 'widow's GMP' of half the member's own GMP (explained above) needs to be paid. However, if the widow was under 45 and had no children, there need be no WGMP.

In 1988 the rights (on the same conditions) were extended to widowers, but only for future and not past service. In 1997, when GMPs were abolished for future service, the rules were changed to say that under the 'reference scheme' the spouse's pension is half the member's own, based on actual service only.

Similarly, for death after retirement, under the 'reference scheme test' (explained on page 36) the spouse's pension is half the member's own. There must be half the member's GMP, for pre-1997 service, for a widow, but for a widower, only service between 1988 and 1997 need be counted.

The widow/er's pension can be taken away if the spouse remarries, or lives with another person as husband or wife.

How contracting out works

With a COSR scheme, it is the *employer* – not the trustees or the individual – who takes the decision on contracting out for the whole scheme. The individual member does not have a choice in the matter. If you did not wish to be contracted out, you would need to leave the scheme.

The 'rebate' (the saving in NI contributions) for an employee is 1.6 per cent of earnings between the LEL and the UEL (explained on pages 4–5). The rebate for the employer is 3.5 per cent of earnings between the limits. The government actuary reassesses these figures, normally every five years.

When SERPS was changed to S2P in April 2002, the Government was lobbied by the pensions industry not to disrupt the contracting out arrangements. Instead, it decided that people in COSR schemes would have an addition to their state benefits, on top of their S2P, to bring them back to what they would have had under the SERPS rules. Only the DWP computer will be able to work this out, but it means that, at least in theory, no one in a COSR scheme will lose out by the change to S2P.

Contracted out money-purchase schemes (COMPs)

If your scheme is money-purchase, it may be contracted out as a COMP scheme. Employers running COMP schemes guarantee to put in at least as much as the NI rebate into the scheme, but there is no guarantee of the amount of pension at the other end. So employees should see a lower amount of NI deduction in their pay because they are contracted out, but then an equivalent amount (or more) going into the scheme.

The rebate is the same for the employee (1.6 per cent of your earnings between the LEL and the UEL), but for the employer it is only 1 per cent. On top of this, all except 16-year-olds have an 'age-related' element, which rises to 10.5 per cent of this band of earnings for the oldest age group. Currently this means people aged 47 and over, but the point at which the maximum is paid rises gradually to 51 and over by April 2006. This money is forwarded to the scheme by the IR after the end of the tax year, but may be delayed if there is doubt about an individual's age.

The percentages above are for April 2002 until April 2007 (when S2P is due to change again). They are higher than the amounts paid before then, because the government is compensating in this way for the changeover from SERPS to S2P (rather than adding something to the state benefit, as with a COSR scheme).

The pension bought by this part of the contribution is called the Protected Rights pension. It must be:

▮ available from age 60 onwards;

▮ all paid as pension, with none being available as a lump sum;

▮ equal for men and women.

The pension set up with the pre-1997 Protected Rights fund has to include provision for a pension for the member's spouse. However, if the member is unmarried at the point when they retire, they can set up a pension without any spouse's rights with the post-1997 money, and be increased each year by a set amount. The rules from 1988 onwards were that the annuities which were bought with the protected rights fund had to increase by 3 per cent or the rise in the retail prices index, whichever was the lower, for years. In 1997 this rule changed to 5 per cent or RPI, and covered the whole of the pension built up after 1997.

The older you are, the less time there is for the pension to build up to give more than SERPS/S2P would provide – or to put it another way, the older you are, the more money needs to be invested to produce the same amount of pension. So, for anyone in their late 40s and above (or younger for women and lower-paid people) there is a risk that contracting out will turn out to have been a bad deal when they retire. Unless the employer is making a high enough contribution to make it pretty certain that people will not lose out, either the scheme is divided into two sections, one contracted in and the other contracted out, with individuals being able to choose between them; or the whole scheme is contracted in, and people can contract out of SERPS/S2P themselves if they want, through a personal/stakeholder pension.

There are very few COMPs, because the rules are cumbersome. Many of the smaller employers who had them have converted instead to GPPs or stakeholder schemes (explained in Chapter 2).

Some larger employers, however, including Siemens and Ford, have COMP schemes which, to complicate matters further, are actually *final-salary* schemes. They get a larger subsidy by this route, rather than the COSR route explained above, and are big enough for the administration not to be a problem.

'Appropriate' personal pensions (including stakeholder pensions)

The third way of contracting out is through an 'appropriate' personal pension (APP). This applies to a stakeholder scheme as well as other personal pensions. This means that the employee and employer pay the full rate of NI contributions and the IR then sends on both the flat rate and the age-related rebate to the APP provider. The rebate is calculated in a complicated way: your earnings are divided into three slices, with a different percentage payable on each. The figures also change year-by-year, up to 2006–07. You can find a full table of the amounts of rebate in the IR's guide CA17 (available on their Web site).

As with a COMP scheme, the pension that builds up from the NI rebates is called the Protected Rights pension. It must:

▮ be available from age 60 onwards;

▮ be all paid as pension rather than a lump sum;

▮ be equal for men and women;

▮ provide a pension for the widow or widower. It must buy the widow/er's pension from the Protected Rights fund but can pay the fund built up from additional contributions as cash. The pension set up with the pre-1997 Protected Rights fund has to include provision for an annuity for the member's spouse. However, if the member is unmarried at the point when they retire, they can set up a pension without any spouse's rights with the post-1997 Protected Rights money;

▮ be increased each year. For pensions built up before April 1997, the whole pension has to be increased by 3 per cent, but for pensions that have built up later, the 5 per cent/RPI rule explained on page 39 only applies to the Protected Rights fund.

Most people with APPs are not paying any extra contributions into their pension, so that all that is going in is the NI rebates. They will not get much of a pension, and will not be able to take a tax-free lump sum on retirement, or be covered for life insurance or ill health insurance.

The older you get, the less likely it is to be worthwhile contracting out. You also need to think about your earnings, especially if it is an older personal pension with high charges. As a rule of thumb, anyone earning less than £10,000 ought to think hard about whether it is worthwhile to contract out.

5 Leaving a pension scheme early

Far more people leave their pension scheme before retirement, or stop paying into a personal/stakeholder arrangement, than ever actually retire from a scheme. What happens to the benefits of these 'early leavers' is, unfortunately, one of the most complicated areas of pensions. The legal rules cover two different aspects: what happens to your pension if you stop being an 'active' member or contributor; and what happens if you want to transfer the pension or the fund that has built up.

Occupational pension schemes

If you have been a member of a scheme for less than two years, you can generally have a refund of your own contributions. The exception is that in a COMP scheme (explained on page 38), you can never have a refund however little time you have been there, and an (often very small) deferred pension has to be set up instead.

Some deductions will be made from any refund. First, since you were given tax relief when the contributions were made, the IR now wants to make sure it gets its money. So your refund is taxed, at a special rate of 20 per cent. Second, if the scheme is contracted out of SERPS/S2P (explained in Chapter 4), there is a deduction to buy you back into the state scheme.

The effect is that you receive back half or less of what you put in. You get no credit for the employer's contributions, which stay in the fund. If your scheme is non-contributory, you have nothing to be refunded, and the employer does not have to offer you a deferred pension either.

If you transfer in service from another scheme, or if you are given backdated service when you sign up to the scheme, this will count towards the time limit.

More than two years' membership: final-salary schemes

After more than two years' membership of the scheme, you must be given a deferred pension, which you can transfer elsewhere if you wish. If yours is a final-salary scheme, this will be calculated on the basis of your pensionable earnings and pensionable service at the time you leave, with increases to take some account of inflation.

Working out these increases (also called 'escalation') is complicated. The pension is divided into several slices, depending on when it was built up ('accrued' in the jargon), because the law has changed several times. The most important change happened in 1997 when, as explained in Chapter 4, the Guaranteed Minimum Pension (GMP) was abolished.

If your scheme was contracted out of SERPS before 1997, the first step is to calculate how much of the overall pension is GMP. This is then increased at a special rate. For most private sector schemes, the figure is 4.5 per cent (compound) each year between the time you leave the scheme and retirement age. It used to be much higher, for those who left in earlier years when inflation was higher – who have now found themselves with a better bargain than they expected. It could well fall further in future, if inflation stays low. For public sector schemes, the increase in the GMP is in line with the rise in the RPI, as it is for the 'excess' pension above the GMP.

In the private sector, however, the 'excess' does not have to keep up with inflation. Instead, the scheme has to give Limited Pension Indexation (LPI), which is either the rise in the RPI or 5 per cent a year compound if that is lower, up until retirement date. The figure is an average, rather than a year-for-year comparison, and is laid down in an Order published by the DWP each year. So, for example, someone who left in 1986 and retired in 2001–02 had their 'excess' pension increased by 80.1 per cent over the 15 years up to retirement.

If your pension scheme was not contracted out of SERPS before 1997, or you have only joined since then, there will be no GMP and so all the pension will be increased in this way.

Information on leaving a scheme

When you leave, you should automatically be given a statement of what your benefits are and what options you have (including the right to transfer, explained in the next section), within two months of leaving the scheme. After that, you have a right to request a new statement, updating the previous one, and to be sent the information within two months. However, the scheme can refuse to supply this if nothing has changed since you last made the request or if it is less than 12 months since you did so.

Transfers

You generally have the right to transfer your deferred pension out of the scheme, up until a year before retirement. (The exceptions are for some cases where you left a scheme before 1986, and when a scheme has got beyond a certain point in being wound-up.) You are allowed to transfer the money to your new employer's occupational scheme, or one or other type of personal pension, or the older form of 'Section 32 buyout' pension policy.

If the pension to be transferred includes a GMP or a Protected Rights pension, some schemes will not be able to accept it, or may say that the GMP element must be left with the old scheme.

The money to be transferred always goes between scheme and scheme, without you ever seeing it. There are some enterprising individuals around who will offer to 'bust' the transfer so you can get the cash – minus a substantial commission for themselves. They will be breaking the law and may well disappear altogether with your money, so it is not wise to get caught up in this.

The money that goes across is called a 'cash equivalent transfer value' (CETV). Essentially, this is the capital that has to be set aside now in order to provide the deferred pension to which you are entitled. It is calculated by the scheme actuary in line with some standard rules.

Joe Average leaves in 2002, with 25 years to go before retirement. His deferred pension comes to £10,000 a year. So the actuary would say, 'He is due annual payments of £10,000 a year starting in April 2027 – how much should be set aside now to produce that?' If we assume that he needs (roughly) £100,000 in the fund by then to provide this, the actuary may then say, 'Well, I consider we can obtain an average of 7 per cent interest on investments each year between now and then.' At 7 per cent interest, with 25 years' growth ahead, he needs around £18,000 set aside now, so this would be Joe's CETV.

If Joe decided to leave his pension in the pension scheme for the moment, but then came back a couple of years later wanting to transfer, the CETV would be larger, because he would be two years closer to retirement and so there would be fewer years' worth of investment return to be included in the calculation. But the assumption is that it would still buy the same pension.

Schemes are allowed to vary the assumptions they use, so that some transfer values will be more generous than others. However, there are several restrictions:

■   The minimum transfer value, for a final salary scheme, is calculated in line with the Minimum Funding Requirement (MFR; see Glossary).

■   Schemes must use the same set of assumptions for transfers in and transfers out (so they cannot be optimistic about investment returns for those they are saying goodbye to, and pessimistic for those they are saying hello to).

■   If there are *discretionary* benefits – that is, if the trustees have the power to give additional benefits, such as extra pension increases – they have to decide whether to take account of these in the transfer value, and tell the scheme members.

Money-purchase pensions (occupational or personal)

With a money-purchase scheme, the starting point for calculating the deferred pension is simply the accumulated fund in your account. The scheme can deduct administrative expenses – but no more than would have been deducted if you were still an active member. In a poor scheme, these may eat up all or most of the money of those who have not belonged to the scheme for long. What's left has to be increased by the same level of investment returns and bonuses as you would have had if you were still an active member.

If your money-purchase scheme is contracted out of SERPS/S2P, your Protected Rights (explained on page 39) fund must be separately accounted for. The detailed rules also changed for these in April 1997, but the principles stayed the same.

The transfer value is simply the amount that is built up in your account, less the charges.

Information and time limits on transfers

When you leave an occupational scheme, you must be told if you have the right to transfer out and where to get further details. If you then ask for an estimate of how much the transfer value would be, you must be given that information within three months (though you can be refused if you have already been given an estimate within the last year). The value is guaranteed for three months. If you accept it within this time, the trustees should pay it over to the new scheme within six months. If they take longer, they must recalculate and pay you either the original value plus interest, or the new calculated value, whichever is higher.

If the scheme is poorly funded, the trustees may decide that they do not have the money to pay full transfer values. They must then explain this to you, and give you the choice of taking a reduced amount or leaving your pension there.

The trustees can also apply to Opra (explained on page 160) for permission to delay paying CETVs – perhaps because a legal dispute means that they are difficult to calculate – but again, they would need to tell the people affected.

Very often you will be offered only a money-purchase pension, not extra years in the new employer's scheme. If you are offered extra years, they may be fewer than you had built up in the last scheme. Most scheme administrators will be reluctant to give advice on whether you should take a transfer in or not (in case you sue them if their advice is wrong). If you feel you need advice, it is best to go to an actuary. The fees can be high, but could well be worthwhile if your pension is valuable.

Transferring to a personal/stakeholder pension

An occupational pension can be transferred to a personal/stakeholder pension. However, advisers must do a 'transfer value analysis' to establish how good an investment return you would need to make a transfer worthwhile, and give you a 'reasons why' letter explaining their advice. To do this, the adviser should ask to see the details of your existing scheme. Be very cautious if the adviser is not interested in this.

6 *Member representation*

Note. This chapter relates mainly to occupational schemes, because most personal and stakeholder pensions do not have trustees, but are managed by an insurance company or other provider. A few, including the TUC scheme, have chosen to have trustees. The overall legal framework for them is the same as for trustees of the other schemes, but there are some additional special rules for them to follow.

Pension scheme trustees

Pensions are a very long-term matter. The youngest member of a scheme may still be drawing a pension in 80 years' time. So you need an arrangement under which the money needed to meet the pension promise is set aside, if that promise is to mean anything. In the UK, the arrangement is the trust fund, under the control of the trustees and legally separate from the employer. The trustees' name says it all: they are being *trusted* to safeguard the benefits.

The trustees are the legal owners of the pension fund and have a duty to act in the best interests of the beneficiaries, that is, all the people who are benefiting from the fund, or might do so in future. They are not there to act as representatives of a group, whether that is management, current employees, or pensioners. The trust must be operated, and the money invested, in line with *trust law.*

Broadly, responsibility for any pension scheme is shared between the trustees and the employer. With the help of advisers, the employer will set up the scheme, decide on the framework of benefits, and draw up the initial trust deed and appoint the first trustees. The employer can also order the trustees to wind up the scheme at any time. But the trustees are responsible for the administration of the benefits, for investing the funds, for seeing that the trust deed is properly adhered to and the commitments to the IR and DWP are met, and for making sure that the funding in the scheme is adequate so that the benefits promised can be delivered. Ultimately, trustees also have the responsibility for closing down the scheme.

The employer can amend the rules of the scheme, but usually only with the agreement of the trustees and only without prejudicing people's existing rights, as explained in Chapter 3. The employer is also responsible for the decision on whether the scheme should be contracted out of SERPS/S2P or not. In some cases the employer has a duty to act in a 'fiduciary' (trustee-like) manner, putting the interests of the beneficiaries above its own. In other cases, the employer's duty is to act 'in good faith', which means that it must consider the interests of the beneficiaries properly, but is then entitled to put its own interests first.

The trustees need to consult the employer about their investment policy, and to agree the contribution levels. They must also consider the interests of the employer *so far as* they relate to the interests of the beneficiaries. If they were to act in an unreasonable way which meant the employer no longer wanted to continue running the scheme, this would not be in the interests of the beneficiaries themselves.

Who can be a trustee?

Anyone aged 18 years and over, and legally capable of holding property, is eligible to be a trustee, except:

∎ anyone convicted of dishonesty or deception;

∎ an undischarged bankrupt;

∎ anyone disqualified from being a company director;

∎ anyone disqualified by Opra from acting as a trustee; and

∎ the scheme's auditor or actuary (although another individual from the firm that the actuary works for, or the firm itself, can be).

Whatever the route by which people have become trustees, once appointed they are all equal. There is no such thing as a first- or second-class trustee. Any facilities that are given to management trustees, like places at conferences, travelling arrangements for meetings or discussions with the advisers, should be given to member trustees as well.

Employment protection and training for trustees

The Employment Rights Act 1996 safeguards the trustees' position against unfair dismissal, or detriment in their employment, for acts carried out as trustees. This applies to any employee who is a trustee – whether member-nominated or not. It means that there is no minimum time for which a trustee need have been employed before he or she can take a case to an Employment Tribunal. The burden of proving that a dismissal was fair falls on the employer, rather than the other way round.

Trustees can claim 'reasonable' paid time off for training and for carrying out their duties. If necessary, the trustee can take a case against the employer to an Employment Tribunal and obtain a declaration and an award of compensation. However, the law says nothing about paying the cost of training.

Action point

All trustees should have a copy of Opra's _Guide for Pension Scheme Trustees_ (see Appendix 2 for details). This includes a list of questions any new trustee should ask about the running of the scheme. New trustees should aim to work through these, perhaps in a meeting with the pensions manager, before their first trustee meeting.

For sources of training, see Appendix 3.

Member-nominated trustees

Sections 16–21 of the Pensions Act 1995 requires at least one-third member-nominated trustees (MNTs) in almost every scheme, _where no alternative has been accepted by the members_. The minimum is two MNTs in schemes with more than 100 members, and one in smaller schemes. There are parallel, and almost identical, provisions for directors of trustee companies (MNDs).

There are exemptions for:

▪ public services schemes and some special statutory schemes, like the one for members of parliament;

▪ schemes providing only death benefits;

▪ schemes that have a statutory independent trustee, because the employer is insolvent.

There are different rules for centralized schemes for non-associated employers, such as industry-wide schemes or those where the insurance company itself provides the trustee, and some special arrangements, laid down in the Acts of Parliament privatizing them, for looking after the schemes set up for employees in the former British Rail and British Coal.

The existing trustees and directors must make and implement 'arrangements' to allow members to select trustees or directors within six months of a scheme being set up. Alternatively, either the trustees or the employer can put forward proposals for 'alternative arrangements', generally called the 'opt-out' process. Most schemes have taken this route.

The trustees or employer must put any proposals to active and pensioner scheme members, and decide whether or not to include deferred members in this. If 10 per cent or more object, they must then hold a ballot between the alternative proposal and the 'prescribed rules'. Alternatively, the employer can then withdraw the proposal and try again with a new or modified one. If a scheme's membership changes substantially (perhaps through a merger or a sell-off) the existing trustees must consider whether they should have a re-run.

The Government has been consulting about new regulations that will make changes to the rules, but has decided to postpone finalizing these, possibly for several years. The proposals are that there will be two possible routes to a member-trustee appointment. Trustees adopting the 'statutory' route will not need to consult scheme members before doing so, and regulations will lay down the procedure they have to undertake.

Those adopting a 'scheme-specific' route will have to consult, and will not be able to use it as a way of avoiding member-trustees altogether, but will have more freedom in designing procedures. When an active member loses his or her job and so becomes a 'deferred member', or retires and becomes a pensioner, it will be possible to remove him or her as a trustee. This would leave it wide open, however, for an employer to remove a troublesome MNT by making him or her redundant.

What to look for

The TUC's policy is that there should be equal numbers of member- and employer-appointees on the trustee board; in practice the best you can get will be 50/50 with the company providing the chair. Employers argue that the company is standing behind the scheme, and so needs more of a say. Logically, this would mean that, in a money-purchase scheme, the employer should not have the majority since it is not taking the risk, but in reality it usually hangs on to the majority.

The design of the procedures for appointing MNTs ought to be 'horses for courses'. In a small company where everyone knows each other, a ballot among all members of the fund is the obvious method. You need to ensure, though, that it is secret, scrutinized by someone whom people trust (if necessary by an outside body) and has its results openly declared, and that the people who go forward for election understand what the job of a trustee is, and especially that it is not a negotiating role.

In a larger company, you may need a more complicated electoral structure to get a fair balance between sites and employment groups. You may not be able to have as many trustees as you have sites, if the committee is to be of a workable size. You'll also have to perform a balancing act between, say, the large site in Manchester and the small one in Wales, or between process and craft workers, to ensure that they will all feel fairly treated.

Example: British Airways

The members of the two British Airways schemes, called APS and NAPS, are divided into constituencies by occupational category. When a vacancy arises, it is advertised and people who want to stand for election need to collect 20 signatures on a nomination form. Ballot papers are then sent out with basic details about each candidate, and counted by a special team with two of the trustees acting as scrutineers. All the papers from an election are kept until the next trustee election in that constituency.

Unusually, the BA rules allow 50 or more members in a constituency to request a ballot to remove a member-trustee from office. There must be a two-thirds majority in the ballot for removal. This did actually happen, in 2001, when the pensioner constituency was very unhappy about BA's proposals to merge the two schemes.

An alternative is indirect election, perhaps via a national joint conference, or a central pensions committee made up of delegates from local committees. Some schemes have joint selection panels, with employer and union representatives interviewing those who have been nominated at local level. It is preferable, though, not to have the employers involved at all in the selection of member-trustees – unless, that is, the members can also be involved in selecting the employer-trustees.

The company may try to dictate that trustees should not be a union or other representative, or that people should give up union jobs if appointed, but you should try to resist. The advantage of having a union representative, or even the convenor, is that he or she will already have arrangements for keeping in close contact with the members. The disadvantages are that representatives are already overloaded with work and may find it difficult to step out of the negotiating role and into the administrative role.

It is useful to reinforce the minimum legal protection in local agreements. Member-trustees can be very vulnerable, since their managers may resent the fact that they are sitting on a board with the top people from the company, and getting to know them a great deal better than the local manager does.

Action points

You and your fellow scheme members, or the union if there is one, may wish to find out what procedure was used in 1996–97 for the appointment of MNTs. In a unionized workplace, the union may have copies of the documents that were circulated; otherwise, ask the pensions manager or administrators.

If you are not happy with these, ask around for details of the sort of arrangements other people have. *Pensions in Practice* (details in Appendix 2) has some useful case-study examples. If you are a union member, ask your union for other examples. They may also have copies of model rules.

Both Opra and the NAPF will be bringing out booklets explaining what needs to be done under the new rules, when they are finalized. Get copies of these and establish what will need to change.

Start discussions with the employer in good time, about what should happen when the new rules come in.

Pension schemes in the public services

The big public service schemes, such as those for the civil service and the health service, do not have trustees or a trust deed. Instead, they were created by Acts of Parliament and then sets of regulations on top. Nor do they all have funds, though what they do varies.

In the Civil Service, the money goes straight out of the taxpayers' pockets into the pensions, through the payroll. This happens also with the armed forces, judges, and members of parliament. For the health service, the teachers and some other groups there are 'notional' (that is, imaginary) funds. The government works out what the value of these would be if it put money in each year, but it does not actually do so. The rules are laid down by statute, after agreement with the unions.

In local government, the rules are laid down in the regulations. There is some flexibility, but overall they are the same for every council. However, there are real funds, run either by the county council or by one district council on behalf of several others: there are 89 different funds altogether. The council as a whole acts in the role of trustee, though it is not legally appointed in the same way as in the private sector. The unions at local level have been able to get 'observer' or 'consultative' status on the council committees that run the investments, though they cannot affect the benefits. Unison has been very active in doing this in many areas – so the best place to start asking what is happening will be the Unison branch.

Advisory and consultative bodies

In addition to member trustees, many employers have set up pensions advisory committees or pension consultative committees. In a large company, some sort of formal communication structure is needed if the trustees are going to keep in touch with the members.

For example, the Pearson Group has pension committees for the main UK businesses, with the composition decided at local level. One of their tasks is to recommend whether any special discretionary increases should be paid to pensioners, above the minimum guaranteed under the rules.

Action points

Any advisory committee can be turned into a talking shop, with everything interesting being referred elsewhere for a decision. It's important, therefore, that:

- members and management on the local committees are given proper training;
- if something goes up to the next level, a decision is reached reasonably quickly and the local committee is informed;
- there is a mixture on the committee of people whose main interest is in pensions and people whose interest is in the more day-to-day problems of the workplace; and
- the different local committees meet together, at least once a year, perhaps at the time when the annual report is issued. This will give people a chance to get to know each other, and also reduce the chances for management to use 'divide and rule' tactics.

---

7 *What sort of pension?*

Do you want your employer to arrange a pension?

The short answer is yes. The state pension is not enough to live on, so to have a comfortable retirement, you need other income as well. Either you finance this entirely yourself, or you persuade the employer to help out. For many people, financing a pension themselves is simply an impossibility. Even if they are reasonably well paid, they have other commitments which mean that paying 15–20 per cent of their earnings, year-in and year-out (which is what it takes to buy a good pension in retirement) is not on. So they need the employer to make a contribution as well.

Having the employer involved, and a collective approach, also means that the pension can be professionally run and invested. Two hundred individuals on their own, each taking out a Personal Pension, are in effect each having to be their own investment expert. Some will get it right, some will get it wrong, but none of them will be able to afford to pay for good expert advice. If on the other hand those 200 people come together in a group scheme, with the backing of an employer, the resources will be there to get the expert advice and administration. The numbers, and the employer's position, create a buying power that can benefit everyone.

Why do employers provide pensions?

To some extent employers feel responsible for seeing that their employees do OK in retirement. This is often described as 'paternalism' but 'partnership', the new buzz-word, is a better way of describing the sort of arrangement that is most likely to benefit people as they retire.

Employers, though, need hard-headed business reasons for having something as expensive and complex as a pension arrangement. Historically, the reasons people always gave for setting up a pension scheme were:

▌ helping with recruitment;

▌ helping retain staff who you did not want to lose;

▌ helping retire staff when it no longer suited the business to keep them on.

How much weight these reasons have depends on the sector, and the occupations, you are dealing with. Where there is a labour shortage, and the employer wants to recruit and hang on to staff with particular skills and qualifications, having good pension arrangements – whether that means an occupational scheme, or paying a substantial contribution into a Personal/Stakeholder scheme – is a definite plus. On the other hand, where the employer is concerned only to drive down costs and recruit at the lowest wages, without worrying about staff turnover, a pension scheme would be seen simply as an unnecessary expense.

Many employers have found the pension scheme particularly useful for easing people out, through offering early retirement rather than making redundancies. If the employer offers a special deal for older workers, the union representatives may well be told, 'Don't stand in our way.'

What sort of pension scheme?

Most employees are in _final-salary_ schemes, explained on page 13, which give them some certainty. Currently, with inflation so low, a pension like this is an inflation-proofed investment whether you stay in the scheme or leave – though if inflation rises above 5 per cent, there will be a ceiling on the inflation-proofing for those in the private (but not the public) sector.

Your pension in these schemes is based on your earnings when you retire, or when you leave the scheme, not on your earnings when you put your contributions into the scheme. You can see how valuable this is if you think back to what you were earning when you first started work, and think about what the difference is. Someone in their 40s or 50s may have seen their earnings multiply by 20 or 30 times during their working lives, in money terms. Prices have gone up vastly also, but most people's earnings – and so also their final-salary pensions – have kept pace with prices or increased faster.

However, providing good and reliable benefits to scheme members is expensive, and the employer is carrying a substantial risk. During the 1980s and much of the 1990s things were going very well for occupational pension schemes, and they were very cheap to run. Now that things are not going so well, employers are becoming increasingly reluctant to provide final-salary schemes, and many existing ones are being closed to new starters. Sainsbury's, Lattice (formerly British Gas) and Marks & Spencer are all companies that have said they are not letting anyone new join their schemes.

Some companies are bucking this trend voluntarily, and others are having to set up final-salary schemes if they want to take on contracts from the public sector (as explained on pages 150–51). The outlook is pretty depressing for getting improvements in that sort of scheme, however, and the running is now being made by money-purchase schemes.

Until recently, people considered money-purchase schemes a poor alternative to final-salary. Because the realities have changed, it is now necessary to accept them, and to focus on the key issues of:

▌ how much money is going in as contributions from the employer;

▌ what sort of choices there are for the members; and

▌ what the insurance company or other provider charges for the scheme.

Of these, by far the most important is the first. Many employers are taking the opportunity of moving from one sort of scheme to the other to cut their contributions in the process. If you can establish a well-financed and well-designed money-purchase scheme, however, it will be worth having. It will, though, shift the balance of advantage. As Bryn Davies put it in his TUC guide, *Getting the Best from Defined Contribution Schemes*:

> a replacement defined contribution scheme that costs the same as an earlier final pay scheme will tend to provide better benefits for the early leaver and worse benefits for the long service member.

Other possible advantages are, Bryn Davies points out:

> ▌ allowing the individual imputation of members' rights, which has the advantage of making it more difficult for employers to surreptitiously cut back on the value of members' benefits, eg when members leave a scheme;

▍ removing any doubt or ambiguity about how funds should be financed and eliminating any possibility of disputes over the use of fund surpluses.

The biggest disadvantage of a money-purchase scheme, even where the employer is putting in sufficient money, is that the member carries the risk if the investments do not do well. Just how big this risk can be was illustrated at the end of December 2001, when for the second year running the stock market ended lower than it had been at the previous year-end. So people could have been putting in contributions over all that time, and seen no increase in the size of the fund they had set aside for retirement. At the same time, because interest rates have fallen, the cost of buying an annuity (explained on page 16) has increased, so your fund buys less income.

There are ways of smoothing out the peaks and troughs in investment returns, but they can only reduce them rather than get rid of them entirely.

Hybrids: getting the employer to carry some risk

The ideal is for the employer to *underpin* the money-purchase benefits, by:

▍ promising a pension of at least x per cent of earnings for each year of service; or

▍ running a two-tier scheme, with a money-purchase pension for younger people, transferring at agreed rates into a final-salary one when they get older; or

▍ (some help, though only a limited amount) guaranteeing the rate at which you can buy an annuity at retirement.

With a good underpin, the individual member can get 'the best of both worlds'. In the good times, members who leave will have the benefit of good investment returns while those who retire will be able to link their pensions to their final earnings. In bad times, everyone will have the earnings link to fall back on.

Negotiating on pensions

Some companies have formal procedures for negotiating on pensions. Others bring together a group specifically created for the purpose when they need to, and have no national-level meetings on a regular basis. Many employers are reluctant to allow negotiation about pensions, even when they accept it on other things, especially if the pension scheme is 'non-contributory'.

The unions have argued for a long time that employment law gave them the legal right to negotiate on pensions, but this was made rather clearer in August 2001, under a decision in the Central Arbitration Committee (CAC) concerning the Union Bank of Nigeria. The bank and trade union Unifi were using the model bargaining agreement set out in Regulations under the 1999 Employment Relations Act, because they had not been able to agree on anything else. This specified 'pay' as one of the items on which the employers must negotiate, and the CAC decided that this included pensions, though not their management or administration.

Negotiating on pensions, when it comes down to it, is like negotiating for any other sort of benefit. You put in a claim for what you think is reasonable, you argue for a while about money, and in due course you reach a settlement which is the best you can get out of the employer at the time. There are, though, certain points that make pensions negotiations different.

First, pensions are more closely bound up with a legal framework than some other things. Second, there will usually be more involvement of 'experts' on both sides. The employer's experts may include the pensions manager, consultant, or insurance company representative. On the other side a number of unions have their own pensions officers, who have a wealth of information and experience at their fingertips. In other cases the unions may employ experts, particularly actuaries, though sadly these do not come cheap.

Pensions negotiations tend to take longer than wage negotiations. Actuaries and lawyers can be very slow. Insurance companies and brokers can be even worse, unless they see a straightforward profit coming out of it for them – as with a brand new scheme. Whether the company generally is centralized or has autonomy at plant level, the pension scheme tends to be very centralized, and controlled by people reporting to the main board. Local negotiations at workplace level are likely to be a waste of time. In some cases, such as the universities, even top management has no power either, because it is an industry-wide scheme and decisions are taken by committees representing all the participants, both the employers and the unions.

It's not easy to achieve a retrospective agreement in the same way as can be done for pay. So you need to start negotiating well before the 'anniversary date' when changes come into force. If any changes mean a computer software programme has to be amended, the deadline may be even earlier!

People will very rarely take industrial action about the pension scheme. They are far more likely to 'vote with their feet' by leaving, or not joining in the first place.

Doing your research

Comparisons are always useful. So do some research on other companies in your industry that are roughly your employer's size. Also check out a different industry, but competing in the same labour market. You could argue, for example, that a firm in Derby that tried to keep its wage rates comparable to Rolls-Royce's in order not to lose workers, ought also to keep its pension benefits comparable.

If you have different pension schemes for white-collar and blue-collar workers, compare those. Look also at the benefits that senior managers are on. The details of these 'top-hat' schemes tend to be kept secret, but you can glean information about their costs, at least, from the company's annual report.

For national comparisons, the most useful publication is the *Survey of Occupational Schemes*, published each year by the National Association of Pension Funds (NAPF). As it is voluntary to take part in the survey, it is probably biased towards the better schemes, but that does no harm! The government actuary also does a big survey every five years. It is much more representative, but takes so long to be published that it is out-of-date before anyone sees it.

Other organizations such as Union Pension Services, Labour Research, and Incomes Data Services also do surveys and case studies, along with individual unions and firms of consultants. Employers' organizations may also send out questionnaires to their own members. If you can get hold of one for your part of industry, this would be well worthwhile.

It is also helpful to have access to the right set of Inland Revenue *Practice Notes* (see Appendix 2), and material from Opra and the Financial Services Authority as necessary.

In the past, all this would have meant spending hours hunting in a library, but so much is now available on the Internet that it is much less of a problem.

8

What makes a good final-salary scheme?

In this chapter we look at what final-salary schemes tend to do, what makes them better or worse and the improvements that can be sought, together with some of the arguments that can be used. The question of cost is obviously important, and this is dealt with at the end of the chapter.

> **Questions to ask about your scheme:**
>
> ▌ Can anyone who wants to, join it?
> ▌ How much do I have to pay in, and how much does the employer pay?
> ▌ How much pension is building up each year?
> ▌ Is all my pay pensionable? If the answer is no, which elements are not?
> ▌ What happens if my pay drops before I retire?
> ▌ Does my whole length of employment count?
> ▌ If I give up part of my pension for a lump sum, how will it be worked out?
> ▌ What age would I normally retire?
> ▌ Can I retire early, and what pension would I get if I do so?
> ▌ What happens if I am made redundant?
> ▌ What if I fall ill and cannot work again?
> ▌ What would be paid out if I died?
> ▌ What happens if I die after retirement?
> ▌ What happens to my pension if I leave?
> ▌ What advice can I get?

Who can join?

Schemes are allowed to let anyone in, from the age of 16 and the day they join the company, until they reach the scheme's normal retirement date (NRD, explained on page 79). A scheme is not allowed, however, to admit a new member who is over NRD. On the other hand, schemes are allowed to close their schemes to new members, to leave it to the trustees or employer to decide whom to admit, or to impose limits on who can or cannot join – so long as they do not break the rules about discrimination explained in Chapter 3.

Around 17 per cent of final-salary occupational schemes in the private sector are closed to new entrants, according to the NAPF's 2001 survey.[1] In many cases, though, there will be another arrangement that new employees can join, which might be a money-purchase scheme or a GPP/stakeholder. Many other schemes have widened their eligibility rules, to exempt the employer from the requirements to provide a stakeholder scheme.

The minimum age for being allowed to join a scheme varies considerably, from 16 in most public sector schemes and quite a large number of private sector ones, to 18 in around a quarter of schemes, up to 30 or higher in a few. Those with a very high joining age may be the upper tier of a two-tier arrangement, perhaps with a money-purchase scheme for younger people.

In just under half of the schemes in the NAPF survey, there was no *maximum* age for joining. Of the rest, 17 per cent had upper age limits of 55 or less, 58 per cent of ages between 56 and 60, and 25 per cent of over 60. Most schemes did not impose a minimum length of service before one could join, and of those that did, in general it was quite short, a year or less.

Some smaller schemes, especially where an insurance company is involved, only let new people in on one date in a year, the 'anniversary date'. This is often 6 April, to coincide with the beginning of the new tax year, and is the date at which premiums to the insurance company are fixed. Some schemes say that if you do not join at your first opportunity, you lose the chance to do so later, or that your case has to be considered individually by the trustees.

Around half of the employers in the NAPF survey provided life insurance to people who were not yet eligible to join the full scheme – in around half of these cases, at a reduced rate compared to those who were full members. This is useful for younger members. It incidentally also allows the employer to claim exemption from providing a stakeholder scheme for these employees, though the DWP has said it will close this loophole if there is evidence of misuse.

How to tell if you are in a good scheme

Membership should be open to the widest possible group, whatever their age and length of service. The argument for this is that if the employer believes the scheme is a good one and worth paying for, then it will be worthwhile for everyone and not just for a selected group. In a more limited scheme, the profits made by the whole workforce are being used to pay for better benefits, and therefore a higher level of deferred pay, for a particular group. Those who see the job as only temporary will probably not join anyway.

In addition, making the pension scheme all-inclusive:

■ avoids the administrative hassle involved in setting up a stakeholder pension scheme and making payroll deductions, perhaps for only a very few people;

■ means that there is no danger that the employer or trustees could fall foul of the laws on equal treatment (see Chapter 3); and

■ has the benefit of bringing in younger people, which is going to improve the scheme's financial health.

A smaller step is to offer life insurance and some contribution towards their personal or stakeholder pension to those waiting to join, so that everyone has some pension coverage. Generally, these payments stop once someone is eligible to join the main scheme, so this acts as an incentive to sign up. Another possibility is to backdate credited service once someone does join, as explained on page 73.

It always has to be voluntary whether to join or leave a scheme. It is preferable, though, to make it automatic for new staff to join, and to explain that they have the right to opt out if they wish.

Saying that people have 'one chance only' to join is hard on people who did the wrong thing when aged 20 and have to live with their mistakes for ever after. However, there does need to be some safeguard against people joining up only when their health begins to deteriorate. One possibility is to say that if people do not join within, say, the first five years of employment, they must satisfy a medical examination before they can join later. Another option is to say that the trustees have discretion about whether or not to admit late entrants (subject, of course, to the Disability Discrimination Act, explained on page 86).

Employers argue that they need minimum ages and/or a waiting period in order to avoid setting up pensions for large numbers of people who then leave. This then leads on to a non-pension issue – what are the causes of high staff turnover, and might having a pension scheme available, as evidence of being a good employer, help to reduce it?

Schemes that require you to work a minimum number of hours before being allowed to join are likely to fall foul of the Part-timer Regulations explained in Chapter 3. Those that say they are only available to 'permanent' staff will need to re-think when the Fixed-term Contracts Regulations, also explained in Chapter 3, come into force.

Some employers may argue that the pension scheme is 'not suit-able' for some groups of staff, perhaps because they are low-paid and the scheme is integrated with the state scheme (explained on page 15). The answer then is to redesign the scheme entirely – as Tesco for example has done – or introduce special provisions. Having a minimum level of earnings before you are allowed to join is questionable under the Equal Treatment rules, because it is more likely that men would be able to meet this requirement than women.

An example

Mrs Shillcock was working for a private school, whose pension scheme excluded anyone whose earnings were below the Lower Earnings Limit (explained on page 15). The school argued that it would not be worth her while joining, because she would receive so little pension. She complained to the Pensions Ombudsman, who said that the scheme should be redesigned so that she *could* benefit, and that excluding her also meant that she was not covered by life insurance, which was valuable however low-paid one was. The case is now going to appeal in the Courts.

Contributions

There's no legal minimum that either the individual or the employer must contribute to an occupational scheme. The maximum allowed by the IR is explained in Appendix 1. While employees get tax relief on their contributions, employers also get theirs treated as a business expense, so they will pay less corpora-tion tax.

The employee's contribution is usually a fixed percentage, but the employer's contribution is generally 'the balance of the cost' of providing the benefits. So it will vary depending on how the scheme's investments are doing and what has been happening to the scheme members. In the past, the employer has often been able to go on 'contribution holiday' – that is, pay nothing in for a while – because the amount already in the funds has been sufficient to cover the cost of the benefits promised. There are schemes that are so well funded, in fact, that neither employer nor employee is making contributions, or will need to ever again.

It is important to look at the pensionable earnings figure – the amount of pay from which the contribution is being deducted (discussed on page 69) – as well as the contribution rate. People in final-salary schemes are paying, on average, between 3 and 5 per cent of pensionable earnings. Some schemes have much higher contribution rates, especially in the public sector. For example, the police pay 11 per cent of pensionable pay. This is because they have especially early retirement dates, and so the scheme is expensive to run. Some schemes, such as BP's, have a tiered contribution rate so that you can pay more and buy extra benefits.[2]

If you are paying more than 3 per cent for a scheme that is contracted in to SERPS/S2P, or 5 per cent for one that is contracted out, you would want convincing that the scheme is good value. You'll also want to know what the employer is paying, and how that compares. Over the long term, a contribution of two or two and a half times the members' own would be about right.

Around a third of all schemes are 'non-contributory' – that is, the member makes no *direct* contribution. The employer pays it all. But really, the money is still coming from the employee – where else is it going to come from? If it were not going into the pension scheme, it would be available to spend on other things, perhaps on wages. So you are still paying.

From the employer's point of view, a non-contributory scheme has the advantage of weakening the negotiating position. Members are, sadly, not so interested in something they feel they are getting 'for free'. So it will be more difficult to persuade the employer to make improvements, or to ensure that member-trustees have real power.

On the other hand, the cost of providing a decent pension is increasing, so employers may well want to bring in contributions where there were none in the past, or to increase the contributions the members are paying. One way of doing this is to give existing members a one-off increase in their pay to offset it, so that they are no worse off but new employees are paying more. Another is to impose the change only for new employees. You and your fellow scheme members might want to suggest that your union presses for a clear increase in benefits, negotiated with the unions, and for any increase in the employer's contribution to be more than that for the members. However, if the employer is strapped for cash, or the cost of the pension scheme has been rising sharply, it would generally be better to give in gracefully rather than see the scheme closed down.

Arguments to use against too high a contribution rate are that:

▪ people will not feel the scheme is value for money, and so the 'public relations' advantage to the employer will be very much reduced;

▪ this will make it difficult to persuade new employees to join, and this will weaken the scheme overall;

▪ the employer's response might be that the members will value the scheme more, the more they pay for it. The rejoinder to this would be that what matters is the *value for money* they feel they are getting, or (especially if it is a new or much improved scheme) that they can only just afford what they are offering to pay now, and any more would 'break the camel's back'.

Accrual rate

This is the rate at which the pension builds up. Look at it alongside the definition of final pensionable pay. Some schemes can look very generous, until you realize that a large slice of the pay is not pensionable.

Usually the accrual rate is given as a fraction of your final pensionable pay for each year of service; common ones are 1/60th, 1/80th, or 1/50th. It could instead be a percentage – 1/50th could be given as 2 per cent, for example. Occasionally it will be given as a total fraction or percentage of your pay after the maximum number of years you can have in the scheme – in a 1/60th scheme, for example, the booklet could say that someone will have two-thirds of their final pensionable pay after 40 years.

There has been a gradual process of improving accrual rates over the years, and now 80 per cent of private sector schemes have an accrual rate of 1/60th, 17 per cent have a higher rate than that (including 5 per cent with 1/30th) and 9 per cent have a lower rate. (The figures come to more than 100 per cent because many schemes have different accrual rates for different sections.) Some schemes have a 1/60th and a 1/80th tier, and may allow people to move upwards but not downwards, or in other cases to move freely. The BP scheme has as many as six tiers, ranging from 1/60th up to 1/35th.[3]

Some schemes, such as ICI's, have different accrual rates for different levels of earnings. In this case, the first £11,520 of earnings accrues at 1/45th, and then it is 1/55th after that (but the scheme is also *integrated*, as explained on page 15).

In the public sector the standard format for many years was to give a 1/80th pension, but then add an automatic lump sum of three times the pension, whereas in the private sector you have to 'buy' the lump sum out of the pension (see pages 77–79 for an explanation).

It used to be argued that this public service formula was roughly equivalent to the private sector 60ths. However, changes in the cost of providing pensions mean that this is no longer true. The new Civil Service pension scheme, which started in April 2002, has an accrual rate of 1/60th.

If your scheme is contracted in to SERPS/S2P

Since you are getting both the state benefit and the occupational scheme (and probably paying for both) it is logical that the accrual rate should be lower. For example, the W H Smith scheme, now closed to new entrants, is 1/95th. Some schemes try to link in very closely with the state benefits, aiming for a 'target' total pension when state and private pension are added together. This is logical, but SERPS/S2P have become so complicated, and been subject to so many changes, that most have abandoned the attempt.

How to tell if you are in a good scheme

If the accrual rate is lower than 60ths, you and your fellow scheme members may want to urge the union that it is worth making an improvement here a priority. If you are looking for a lower retirement age, you may well want a better accrual rate as well, so that people can earn as much pension as before, but in a shorter time. The automobile industry, for example, has several schemes with a 1/50th accrual rate, since most people will retire well before 65.

Apart from comparing your scheme with others in the industry, arguments would be: with the state basic pension falling in real value, a low accrual rate means that anyone with less than 40 years' service will not have enough to live on; and because the Government is planning to means-test more and more pension-ers' income, people who end up with a low pension may have poor value for money out of their contributions and those of the employer.

If you can't get your accrual rate improved all at once, it might be possible to have a change phased in over several years.

'Integrated' pension schemes

What these are, and how they work, was explained on pages 15–16.

Around half of all members of private sector schemes are in inte-grated schemes. The most common level of earnings to be excluded is once times the basic state pension/LEL, with around 50 per cent of the members having this arrangement.

This reduces the benefits below what they would be in a scheme that was similar but non-integrated. The lower-paid you are, the bigger the reduction. If senior managers, shopfloor workers and part-time staff are all in the same scheme, the highest-paid people will hardly notice the effect, while the worst-off will be badly hit. This raises questions of indirect discrimina-tion. In many companies, the majority of the lower-paid group and the majority of part-timers, will be women. The scheme rules could therefore be in breach of the Equal Treatment rules, explained in Chapter 3.

To reduce this impact, many schemes pro-rata the integration factor for part-timers. This means that they reduce it in proportion to the number of hours someone is working, compared to a full week. For instance, someone doing only half the standard hours would have a deduction of only half the LEL. Alternatively, the deduction may be limited to, for example, 12.5 per cent of pay. This sort of adjustment can reduce the worst features of integration, but do not stop it being unfair.

If the pension formula is integrated, the contributions should be also. This would mean that, when the contributions are worked out, they will only be on the slice of pay above the integration factor.

People tend to be misled by integration, although the pensions industry will claim that it is all spelt out in the scheme booklet. Many scheme booklets use worked examples, but it would not be uncommon for the example of the pension calculation to say some-thing like, 'A's final pensionable earnings are £15,000, and so 40/60ths of that is £10,000', without explaining how the final pensionable earnings figure has been reached. The information will be there somewhere in the booklet, but often it is only in the list of definitions, on a separate page at the beginning or end of the booklet, not where the member needs it. Some integration arrangements are so complex that people find it very difficult to work out their pension at all.

The ICI scheme for example gives a pension of 1/45th of earnings on the first £11,250, and then 1/55th above that, but then reduces it by 1/50th of the basic state pension for each year you have been in the scheme.

Trade unions, especially Unifi and MSF, have been campaigning against integration (or 'clawback' as they usually call it) for many years. They have asked MPs to raise the issue in Parliament, and had demonstrations about it. One recent example of a change was in the Ocean Nestor Pension Scheme, which in 2001 swept away integration and gave special increases to those already on pension to remove the effect of it, as if it had never been.[4]

If it is not possible to have the integration factor abolished altogether, or if people would not like a sudden jump in contributions, a first step is a freeze in the deduction at its current money value. As time goes on, it can be cut down and finally abolished altogether. That way, no one will pay more in a sudden jump, but the effects will be very much reduced. Another possibility is a formula that safeguards the lower-paid in particular.

For example, the British Steel (1990) Pension Scheme says that 'if your gross earnings are less than 4 times the annual state flat-rate pension for a single person for that year, Pensionable Earnings will be taken as 75 per cent of your gross earnings'.[5]

Bridging pensions

Many integrated schemes include a 'bridging pension' for early retirement. This is because someone who retires earlier than state retirement age will not be able to draw the state pension that has been included in the pension calculation. So schemes may offer either an extra temporary pension, often equivalent to the state basic pension, but which stops when the state pension comes into force, or a 'level pension option'. This means that the individual can opt to draw a larger pension before state pension age, and a smaller one thereafter. The aim is that, on average, there should be no cost to the scheme. This is gambling on your own life expectancy, as someone who lives to the age of 100 on a permanently reduced pension will have had a very much worse bargain than someone who lives only to 70.

Levelling options are therefore much less satisfactory than bridging pensions. Neither, though, provides equal treatment for men and women, as they will be paid up to 65 for a man but only 60 for a woman. In a 1994 legal case, *Roberts v Birds Eye Walls*, the European Court decided this was not unlawful.

Pensionable and final pensionable earnings

'Pensionable earnings' are used to work out members' benefits and contributions. They may not be the same as actual earnings, either because they leave out some parts of your pay or (occasionally) because they include 'notional' figures for something that is not there. For a final-salary scheme, there are also *final* pensionable earnings, the figure actually used to calculate your pension when you retire or leave.

Scheme rules can make any parts of pay 'pensionable' or 'non-pensionable', so long as, if the scheme is contracted out of SERPS/S2P, it still passes the 'reference scheme test' explained in Chapter 4. The IR rules for what can be counted as earnings are explained in Appendix 1.

While some people have simply an annual salary, others have pay packets made up of several different elements. These might include the basic wage, overtime, performance-related bonus, or shift premium. Some people do not have a basic wage at all, but are paid entirely on piecework. Some items, like bonuses and overtime, may be regular and contractual, or they may be very irregular. In some workplaces with a continuous process, almost everyone on the shopfloor will be on a shift pattern, while in other places there may be many day workers, and people coming up to retirement tend to stop doing shiftwork.

For pension schemes, however, common formulas are:

▌ annual rate of basic pay;

▌ annual rate of basic pay, plus bonus and shift premiums, but not overtime;

▌ basic pay over the last year, plus 'fluctuating emoluments' (explained above) over the last three years;

▌ PAYE earnings over the last tax year.

How to tell if you are in a good scheme

The pensionable pay should be the pay that people are likely to get when they are at or near retirement. It should include the *steady* elements of pay, such as regular shift premiums, contractual overtime and guaranteed bonuses. Windfalls and payments such as occasional overtime should not be included.

It's possible to have a formula that 'irons out' the fluctuations between payments to individuals, and the different levels of overtime. This can be done by fixing a multiple of basic pay – for instance, 1.25 times or 1.33 times, which is used as a notional pensionable pay figure. This must, however, be a realistic average for people's regular earnings, otherwise you could find individuals come up against the IR's limits (see Appendix 1).

In a career average scheme like Tesco's (explained on page 14) or a good hybrid one, people will get most benefit from having all earnings included, since people will get full value for contributions made at any time in their working career.

The same definition should be used for contributions and for pension benefits; but for the death benefit, *all* earnings should be included.

If you have a change in the pay arrangements, for example moving to annualized hours, the employer should check how this affects pensions and make special arrangements to safeguard them if necessary.

It's quite straightforward for the booklet to include several definitions. It might, for example, make sense to use basic pay for those on staff terms and conditions, and PAYE for shopfloor workers. In companies with a lot of different workplaces and different wage payment systems, it may be best to leave the precise definitions to local agreement within some broad guidelines.

If there is a grade rate that relates fairly well to what people actually get, or an average for the work group, you could use that to provide a 'notional' rate, where someone has been off sick for some time.

If there is an improvement in the pensionable earnings formula, it will probably mean more money being collected in contributions as well. It is wise to find out how the scheme members would feel about this before agreeing, and to put some effort into communicating the reasons. The cost to the employer will also increase, of course, which is why they may be reluctant to agree to the change.

Final pensionable earnings

The simplest pension scheme will base the pension on the figures for the last tax year (April to April) or the last 12 months. More often, a scheme will take:

▪ the annual average of the last three years' earnings;

▪ the annual average of the best three consecutive years' earnings in the last 10 (or 13) years' earnings;

▪ 'the best two years in the last five', or even the average of the last five.

In the past, people generally earned most in their last year, or their last few years, because the effects of inflation cancelled out any drop in the amount of overtime or shiftwork they were doing. With pay rises now so much smaller, it is useful to have a formula that can pick up years of better earnings in the past. However, mathematically the *average* of say, three years, is always going to be lower than the best single year. If your scheme is based only on basic pay, it is best to have the best single year's pay in the last 10 (if possible revalued to take account of inflation) as the formula.

Smiths Industries, for example, says that final pensionable earnings are the 'highest consecutive 12 months or 52 weeks of basic salary in the last 10 years of pensionable service'. The IR may not allow this, however, in a scheme that includes 'fluctuating emoluments' like overtime or commission. An alternative is to say, as for example in the Stagecoach scheme, that the final pensionable earnings are 'the greater of member's pensionable pay at the date of retirement or withdrawal from service; or member's highest average pensionable pay in any three consecutive years over the last 10'.[6]

One disadvantage of including overtime and shift premiums is that members may decide to work far longer hours than they should, as they come up to retirement, in order to maximize their pensions. Excessively long and unsocial working hours, for someone in his or her 50s or 60s, are a pretty good way of reducing life expectancy.

To reduce the dangers of this, some schemes say that these elements are always averaged over three years, or that sudden jumps in their size in particular years (say, more than a 20 per cent increase in the level of overtime payments) will be ignored for the purpose of calculating the pension. Another way of dealing with shift premiums is to give extra credited service, as in the Dunlop Tyres example on page 73.

The more expensive the employer says that a change of this sort will be, the more unsatisfactory the formula must be now.

Action point

You and your fellow scheme members might like to suggest that the union representatives work out examples to show what difference it would make. They could ask particular individuals coming up to retirement to let themselves be used as examples, or use workplace average earnings. The point to stress is that this is *not* a final earnings scheme, when you were told it was. The scheme members are being misled.

The employer may say that it will be too complicated to work out, especially if you are asking for the earnings figures to be revalued to take account of inflation. This is not so, because the figures have to be collected anyway. It is simply a matter of making a different use of them. Alternatively, the employer may say (the real reason) that it will cost too much. If you can obtain the figures for this, you and your fellow scheme members can decide how important this is.

Pensionable service

This means the length of your employment that is used in the calculation to work out your pension. Some schemes give you a pension only for complete years in the scheme. This means that unless the scheme's anniversary date happens to coincide with your birthday, you could be paying in contributions for anything up to 51 weeks for no benefit. Better schemes allow you to count the months, weeks and even days of service.

Aim at least for complete months to be added, even if you accept that extra weeks might be too difficult to cope with. You should not have to pay contributions for any service for which you are not building up pension.

Maximum service

Some schemes have a 40-year maximum service rule. Others have a higher accrual rate (explained on pages 65–67) and a shorter service maximum. So, for instance, a scheme with a 50ths accrual rate might have a maximum of 33 years' service to count.

These limits are only ever going to affect a few people, since most of us do not get the opportunity to work for one firm throughout our working lives, so cost barely comes into it. The aim should be to have no maximum service limits, except those required by the IR.

This gives you and your fellow scheme members the chance of turning on its head the employer's argument that they want to 'reward loyalty'. Why should people be penalized for being *too* loyal to the company? The employer may say that they see this level of pension as 'correct'. This is not logical, because most people will get less as they will not have worked for the company for long enough. If it is acceptable for their level of pension not to be correct, why not those who have worked longer than the 'correct' length of time?

You could also suggest that if the employer is concerned about people obtaining 'too much' pension because they have worked too long, those who have reached the maximum number of years could retire before they get to scheme retirement age, without their pension being reduced at all.

Credited years

Some schemes with age or service qualifications credit extra service once you are eligible to join the scheme. So, for instance, the scheme might only allow people in at the age of 20, but credit them with service back to 18. This means that the employer does not have the trouble of collecting and refunding small amounts of contributions for youngsters who did not stay very long, but that people can still build up a reasonable level of pension.

A few schemes give extra years to take account of shiftworking, or to keep up the value of the pension to people whose earnings have dropped perhaps because of redeployment.

In the Dunlop Tyres scheme, the pension is worked out first using a formula excluding shift pay. Then a separate element is worked out taking account of all the shiftwork the member has done over his or her working life, even if he or she is no longer doing it. People can quite easily accumulate three or four extra years' pensionable service in this way.[7]

This sort of arrangement could be used much more widely than it is. The arguments in favour are that unless something like this is done, people will have been contributing towards a benefit they will not in fact receive; if their pay has been reduced, they are already making a sacrifice in terms of their day-to-day living standards, and should not be asked to make a further one in their pension.

As usual, the employer's arguments will be about cost and complication. However, the company has to keep proper records of past payments and working patterns anyway – not just for the IR, but also in case of any legal claims in the future – so this will not add very much to the complication. If it is too complex to go into the ordinary pension calculation programme, it can be done as a stand-alone one for those it particularly affects.

Gaps in employment

The rules about pensions and maternity and parental leave were explained in Chapter 3. Not many schemes do anything more than is legally required, except in the public sector. In local government, for example, people on unpaid maternity leave are allowed to continue paying in contributions while they are away, at the same rate as if they were on normal pay, and this period will then count fully for pension. For other forms of leave, sickness tends to be better treated than, for instance, sabbaticals.

There is generally an advantage from the member's point of view in staying in the scheme, even if no pension is building up. It means that the period of service before and after the break can be counted as continuous, so that the total pension is based on your final earnings at retirement; otherwise, there will be a deferred pension for the first period of service. However, if someone returns to work part time or on a lower grade, so that his or her pensionable earnings were substantially lower, it could be better to treat the two periods of service separately. Since these cases will be uncommon, it should be possible for the scheme administrator to check the circumstances in each case and offer individuals the best option.

An employer may not want to keep someone in membership of the scheme during a long absence because it could also mean maintaining his or her contract of employment. However, anyone who is away because of sickness should be kept in the pension scheme and therefore covered for death benefit – which could be very important for them – for as long as they are kept on the payroll.

If there is a special deal for, say, career breaks or sabbaticals to do voluntary work, pensions should be covered as part of it. In a good agreement, service will be treated as continuous, or as two separate periods, depending on which is more favourable to the member, and life insurance will continue at the rate it was when he or she stopped paying into the scheme.

The argument for this would be that absences that were authorized or encouraged by one department should not be penalized by another. Being generous on this aspect is unlikely to be very expensive, because few people will be affected at any one time. The Government is pressing employers to improve the 'work/life balance'. Offering good arrangements for breaks, whether for family or education reasons, is one way of doing this.

Industrial action

A few schemes, especially those in the public sector like local government and the teachers' scheme, have special rules about strikes and other industrial action. These tend to be fairly punitive: the LGPS guide, for instance, says that if you are not paid for a period of unauthorized absence, this period will not count towards your pension. However, if the unauthorized absence was because of an industrial dispute, you can count it as a period of membership if you pay 16 per cent of the pay you would have received during the period of absence. The amount you have to pay for this period is set out in the rules that control the scheme, and is higher than normal because you have to pay the contributions that your employer normally pays.

Most industrial disputes are not long enough to make much difference to the pension. If you are involved in a long one, however, and the issue is not covered in your scheme, ask your union to try to negotiate on the pension while settling the dispute. The most the employer is likely to concede is that people can have the period of service counted if they pay both the employer's and employee's contributions for that period. The union ought to look for a long period of time to pay those contributions off, and also try to ensure that anyone in the last few years before retirement is not penalized by the way final pensionable earnings (explained on page 71) are calculated.

Backdating service

Backdated service might be offered where the employer is forced into it by legal requirements such as those on Equal Treatment (explained in Chapter 3). It might also arise when a new scheme is replacing an old, rather worse one, and the employer wants you to transfer all your money in.

It has always been very unusual to get full past service where there was no scheme before. It would be even rarer now than in the past, because the new accounting standards (called FRS17, and explained on page 183) would mean that the company had to show the full costs in their accounts in that year, which might wipe out their profits entirely. It might be possible, though, to get credit at a reduced rate for previous years – for example, 120ths in a 60ths scheme.

Backdated credits of this sort benefit most those who have been with the company the longest. If the company or the workplace is fairly new, you and your fellow scheme members may not feel they should have much priority (though it would not cost much to provide them). On the other hand, if there is a large group of long-serving members who are going out of the door with little or no pension, they at least may feel it is very important.

Even a smaller fraction is better than nothing. If the company refuses even that, one possibility is a phased approach. For instance, this might say that anyone retiring in the next 10 years, with 10 years' service or more, should have credits given to make up their pension to the 10 years' level. Some companies have reduced the cost in the opposite way, by limiting the rights of members who retire in the first few years of the scheme. This is not a good idea, as it gives least to those who need it most. The argument in favour is that it is unfair for the company to make provision for the future, without being prepared to do something for those who have already given their working lives to the company.

You cannot be contracted out of SERPS/S2P retrospectively.

Discontinued schemes

Many large employers will have some very poor old schemes, perhaps giving a flat rate pension per year of service tucked away somewhere, which they would like to tidy up. Crediting the members with extra service in the current scheme is the best answer, but the least the company should do is to increase the frozen benefit by the amount by which prices have risen since the date the scheme was frozen, and then either increase it at a fixed rate, or keep it in line with inflation. Alternatively, they could put a lump sum into the members' pension, or their AVC account (see page 118) to 'buy-out' the old pension. It will be important that the scheme members, or their union, obtain actuarial advice, or get the scheme's actuary to go through the calculations in detail, to ensure that a fair deal is being given.

Again, it will be older people with longer service in the old scheme who suffer most by having old benefits frozen. Although there is now some inflation-proofing for early leavers' benefits, this is only in line with prices, and earnings can be expected to rise faster, so they are losing out. Some of these frozen benefits may in any case date from days before there was proper inflation-proofing for early leavers. Paying for deferred pensions was in the past very easy. In fact, they effectively subsidized the rest of the benefits in the scheme, because they were increasing by only a low percentage while interest rates and returns on investments were much higher, so people are owed some credit for the past.

Lump sums on retirement

Most pension arrangements allow people to take a lump sum on retirement, but they can do this in three different ways:

▌ it may be the only benefit the scheme offers;

▌ it may be in addition to the pension; or

▌ it can be on offer to those who want to give up part of their pension in return.

Giving up part of an occupational pension is called 'commuting it'; in effect, your pension is calculated, and you then sell part of it for the lump sum. How this works, and the IR limits, are explained fully in Appendix 1; here we give a basic outline, using an example.

An example: Patricia

Patricia's earnings, in her last year before retirement, are £16,000. She has worked for the company for 30 years, and it is a 1/60th scheme. Her scheme rules say provided a member has more than 20 years' service, they can have 1.5 times their earnings as a lump sum; 1.5 times 16,000 is £24,000 – the amount she can take as a lump sum.

Some other schemes will start with the pension, and say that she can have 2.25 times her pension as a lump sum: 30/60ths of £16,000 is £8,000. Multiplying that by 2.25 gives her £18,000.

A second question is how much pension you have to give up in return for the cash – in other words, how much you are 'selling' your pension for. In Patricia's case, her scheme says that for every £12 in cash, she loses £1 of pension. So if she takes £24,000 cash, she will lose £2,000 of pension, leaving £8,000 to live on.

Pension schemes are allowed to discriminate between men and women in terms of the amount of lump sum they give for each £1 of pension given up, and many do. For once, it is women who do better. Women's average life expectancy is longer, so they can expect their pensions to be paid for longer. Since they are giving up more, they are compensated by a higher amount.

In the private sector, most occupational schemes follow the IR limits on the maximum you are allowed to take as a lump sum (explained in Appendix 1), though there are still a few with tighter restrictions. Most, though, offer less than they could as the 'buy-out' figure – usually called the 'commutation rate'. One recent survey found that only two out of 31 schemes were using the IR's enhanced rates, with all the rest below this. Some used the same rates whatever age the member, even though a younger person – who can expect to live longer on pension – is giving up more.

There was a very big difference between the best and the worst rates, partly because of the difference in the benefits being given up. Shell's Contributory Pension Fund, at the top of the league, gives a woman £14 for every £1 given up at age 65, and £20.16 at age 50. For men, the figures are £11.62 and £17.75 at those ages. This is, though, a scheme that increases pensions in line with the RPI up to 7 per cent a year (so people are giving up a lot). Among the schemes using unisex rates, BBA gave £12.31 at 65 and £17.23 at 50, for both sexes.

At the bottom of the league, it is more difficult to say who is worst because the position varies according to the age of the person concerned. Putting together the worst rates, though, they were £11.82 for a woman of 65, or £13.40 for a woman of 50 (£10.20 and £12 for a man) or £9 at 65 and £10.30 at 60 for the schemes using unisex rates.

These rates would make a big difference to how much pension you kept in your hands. Taking the example of Patricia above, and assuming she was retiring at 65, for her lump sum of £24,000, at Shell she would need to give up £1,714 pension (£24,000 divided by £14). Taking that away from her total pension of £8,000, that would leave her with £6,286 a year to live on. At the scheme with the worst rates for a woman of 65 (Kodak) she would need to give up £2,030 (£24,000 divided by £11.82). That would leave her only £5,970 to live on.

A number of schemes have reviewed their rates in the recent past, according to this survey. Scottish Amicable, for example, which uses the same rate regardless of sex or age, changed this from £10 per £1 to £12 per £1 in 2000. John Lewis increased all the rates by £1, so that for example, at age 60 the rate improved from £11 per £1 to £12 per £1.[8]

How to tell if you are in a good scheme

The scheme should not make a profit from commutation. You and your fellow scheme members might like to ask the employer, or the trustees, to get figures from the actuaries about what would be the fair rates. If they are using the same rate for all ages, ask about the fair rates for all ages down to 50. If the rates being used are unfair, then currently there is a hidden subsidy to the employer's contribution rate. This means that improving commutation will involve a cost – though how much will depend on how big the change is.

Other than cost, the employer's arguments would be, first, paternalism: 'People will get this big lump sum, and may spend it unwisely.' There *is* an argument that given current rates of return on investments, it is actually better not to commute the maximum but to leave it in the pension scheme.[9] But that is for the individual to decide.

The second argument would be inertia: they don't want to go through the bother of changing the rules. So much is changing in pensions these days, however, that there will certainly need to be other rule changes at some point, so they can do several at once.

Retirement ages

In the public sector, just under half of all scheme members have age 65 as the Normal Retirement Date (NRD) and the rest have age 60. In the private sector, around a third have age 60, 58 per cent have age 65, and most of the rest have odd different ages in between. Only 1 per cent has an NRD below 60. Some employers, for instance, decided at some point to 'split the difference' between men and women and have an NRD of 62.[10]

In many companies, very few people retire at NRD; most take early retirement instead. Even so, the NRD is important, because how much you can have as a pension will often depend on how long you have to go until the scheme's retirement age.

How to tell if you are in a good scheme

Most people would want their scheme to let them retire, on a full pension, at 60 or even sooner. This is not uncommon in areas like financial services, but much less so in manufacturing. Over the last decade, in fact, we have seen women's NRD rising to 65, rather than men's falling. If this is accompanied by extra flexibility to take early retirement on good terms, however, it need not matter. Formally lowering the NRD is expensive, and most employers prefer to keep control by offering special deals when it suits them, and then shutting off the tap when the labour market is tight. However, if you can see that most people are actually retiring at a younger age than NRD, it is better if this is put into the rules and does not depend on the whim of the employer.

There can, though, be a downside to reducing retirement age. In a good scheme, benefits such as ill health pensions and dependants' benefits are calculated to include credits for your 'prospective' service – years you could have worked but have not. So for instance, someone going at 55 would have 10 years' prospective service credited if their retirement age is 65, but only five years' if it is 60. It's best, therefore, if a reduction in retirement age happens at the same time as an improvement in the accrual rate.

Early retirement

Note. Ill health retirement is dealt with in the next section. This one covers voluntary early retirement and early retirement due to redundancy/severance.

Schemes do not have to have any rules about early retirement – though most do. The minimum they have to pay, when it is allowed, is the 'actuarial equivalent' of the deferred pension the employee would be entitled to at NRD as an early leaver (see Chapter 5). That is, the actuary works out:

▌ what you would be due under the rules at, say, 65;

▌ what the capital cost of buying that pension would be;

▌ how much pension can be bought at the age you want to retire, say 55, with the same amount of money.

If you have a GMP (explained on page 37), the actuary also has to be sure that enough money will be available in the scheme when you reach state retirement age, to pay your entitlement then. In some schemes, many people will not be able to take early retirement at all, because their early retirement benefits fall below GMP levels. In more generous schemes, an early retirement pension is paid and then the shortfall is made up at 60 or 65.

There is usually a considerable gap between what you can have if *you* choose to retire (often, not a lot) and what you will get if the employer wants you to go. For those going of their own accord, many schemes provide a pension based only on actual service, and current earnings at the time of retirement, and then impose an 'actuarial reduction'. This reduces the pension by a percentage for each year, or month, by which the member retires early. The idea behind this is that there is less money in the fund at that stage for the member to draw on, and the pension is likely to be paid for longer.

However, in many schemes the full actuarial reduction – which is around 9 per cent of pension for each year you are going early – may not be imposed. Instead, the pension may be reduced by:

▌ 0.5 per cent per month by which retirement is early (6 per cent per year);

▌ 0.33 per cent per month (4 per cent per year); or

▌ 0.25 per cent (3 per cent per year).

Increasingly, schemes include a 'no-reduction band' – that is, the rules say that someone retiring between 60 and 65 will not suffer an actuarial reduction. Other schemes impose a 'rule of 85', or a similar figure – that is, if a member's age and service together add up to 85, they can take early retirement with no actuarial reduction. This means that a 60-year-old with 25 years' service can take early retirement, while a person of the same age with shorter service cannot, or only with an actuarial reduction.

In many schemes, you must have the employer's consent before an early retirement pension can be paid. This is for a rather sneaky financial reason. Having the *right* to retire at 60, rather than 65, is a valuable addition to the benefit – since the pension will be paid for five years longer. So it increases the cost of giving you a deferred pension or a transfer value (explained in Chapter 5). If it is only an option, to be exercised by the employer rather than by you, these calculations can assume that you will not draw the pension until 65.

As explained on pages 67–69, an *integrated* pension scheme may offer a 'level pension option' or a 'bridging pension' to early retirees.

Retirement 'at the employer's request'

This includes redundancy arrangements, severance packages and one-offs where perhaps your face doesn't fit. (*Your Rights at Work* details your employment rights; see Appendix 2.)

The employer is essentially trying to buy you out of your job, so usually there will be no actuarial reduction. Often the pension is also increased to take account of potential as well as actual service; this could take the benefits up to the IR limits (explained in Appendix 1). This sort of increase may not be included specifically in the scheme rules or the booklet, however. Often employers find it useful to make a 'special offer', with a time limit, so that all those taking up early retirement during that time receive the improved terms.

Many of the massive pension surpluses in the very big schemes run by the old nationalized industries – British Gas, Electricity Supply, British Telecom and so on – were used up by paying out big early retirement pensions while their workforces shrank. In effect, people were bought out with their own money.

People are often given the choice of an increased early retirement pension, or a redundancy payment that is larger than the statutory minimum. One advantage of this is that the lump sum from the pension scheme does not count against the £30,000 tax-free limit for severance payments. If a trade-off is not on offer, it may be possible to arrange with the scheme administrator to have your severance payment paid into the scheme instead, to increase your pension. There are special IR rules about how you do this, however, and the money must pass from the employer to the scheme direct, not via you, to get the maximum tax benefit.

Legally, the employer can offset a pension against the *statutory minimum* redundancy payment if the person is going within 90 weeks of normal retirement age, but this is hardly ever done.

Good early retirement provisions make a scheme expensive, because the contributions have had less time to build up investment returns, and the pension will be paid for longer. It is not just that you are drawing it five or 10 years before it was expected – you may well draw it for longer, because if your job was unhealthy or stressful, your life expectancy could go *up* when you retire.

People often underestimate the amount of money they will need to live on for perhaps 30 years of retirement, and come to regret it. The way the state benefits system works also means that small amounts of early retirement pension may give you very little extra income. At the same time, however, if the pension scheme is doing well, it should be used to improve benefits overall, not to allow the company to cut jobs without paying the true cost.

How to tell if you are in a good scheme

A good scheme will offer as attractive a pension as possible when a person retires, as of right, without the need for the employer to consent or picking and choosing who gets it, and with the cost coming out of a department's operating budget, as an additional contribution to the pension scheme, not out of any surplus in the fund.

More specifically, there should be no actuarial reduction for early retirement, or as low a one as possible. A 3 per cent reduction for each year by which you are going early, may be a reasonable target. To achieve flexible retirement, there should be an age-band with no reduction at all, between 60 and 65.

Ideally, credited service if someone is going on severance/redundancy should be written into the scheme rules, but in practice the employer will probably want to have it on offer at certain times and not others.

Individuals should be given a reasonable chance to consider the early retirement option, and have the chance of a discussion with a financial adviser, paid for by the company, to go through what it means.

Ill health retirement

This may also be called 'incapacity', 'invalidity', or 'disability' retirement. As an alternative to having special provisions in the pension scheme, many employers have a separate insurance policy, called 'permanent health' or 'income protection' insurance (PHI or IP). These are dealt with in Chapter 9, since they are particularly common with money-purchase schemes.

Occupational pension schemes do not have to have any rules about early retirement of any sort. The rules if they are contracted out of SERPS/S2P are the same for ill health retirement as for any other early retirement. See page 6 for details of how state benefits are affected by income from a pension or an insurance policy.

Over half of all members in the private sector, according to the NAPF survey, are in schemes that give the full prospective pension on ill health:[11]

> Jim is aged 45, and has been a member of his good-quality scheme for 10 years. Scheme retirement age is 65. So if he has to go on ill health grounds, his pension is calculated on the basis of his 10 years' actual service, plus 20 years' prospective service, making 30 in all.

Other schemes give credit for some prospective service, but not the full amount. The public sector has a pattern of its own. The major schemes all give a partially increased pension for those who have completed five years' service, calculated as:

▪   service between five and 10 years is doubled;

▪   service between 10 and 13.33 years is made up to 20 years;

▪   service over 13.33 years has six and two-thirds years added.

However, the extra service must not take you above the scheme's retirement age.

How schemes define 'ill health' also varies. For half the members in the private sector, and 61 per cent in the public sector, the NAPF survey[12] found that it was roughly the same definition as the IR one quoted on page 166. Forty-six per cent of members in the private sector and 9 per cent in the public sector, however, were in schemes with a tougher definition: that you must be unable to do any job at all before you qualify.

There may also be a tiered arrangement, with a more generous pension for those who are seriously disabled than for those incapacitated from doing their own job, but still able to earn something.

In parts of the public sector, such as teaching and local government, the Government has taken the view that the ill health rules have been abused, and have pushed through a considerable tightening up of procedures and definitions. For example, the local government employers have been pursuing an 'action plan'. As a result:

▪   since 1997 the regulations have said that ill health retirements must be certified by an independent medical practitioner, approved by the appropriate administering authority;

▪   from 1 July 1999 these independent medical practitioners certifying ill health retirements were required to be qualified in occupational health medicine; and

▪   from 20 May 1999 the criteria for ill health retirement were extended to include 'any other comparable employment'.

A very public plan like this would be rare in the private sector, where it would be more a matter of management directives coming down from the top level, but these are certainly being given.

It may be the trustees or the employer who actually takes the decision on whether someone qualifies for ill-health retirement, depending on the rules of any particular scheme. They may simply be *required* to ask for medical advice, or be *bound* by that medical advice. In practice, often the trustees do not follow the rules properly, for instance allowing the company's in-house doctor, or human resources director, to dictate to them.

Ill health retirements *are* expensive, and no one would support people being 'written off' as unfit to work when they are perfectly capable of doing so. However, it is very important that the definitions and processes are applied fairly and impartially.

On the one hand, it is not unknown for senior managers to be retired early 'due to ill health' when the company has really decided that it does not want them in the job. At the other end of the scale, the cases which go to OPAS and the Pensions Ombudsman (explained on page 155) are, hopefully, examples of particularly bad practice rather than typical. But they do show that even highly 'respectable' companies can treat people very unfairly on ill health retirement.

In one case, an insurance company refused someone a pension after he had decided against having an operation that the in-house doctor believed would cure his problems. The Ombudsman's report said that:

> I concluded that the insurer had been dictatorial and arrogant and had no right to push the complainant into having an operation, particularly when he had consulted specialists who advised against it, and to refuse him a pension when he did not comply.'[13]

How to tell if you are in a good scheme

There should be no qualifying period for ill-health retirement, or no more than 12 months at most. If there already is a qualifying period before someone can join the scheme, there ought not to be another on top of that.

The definition of ill health should allow you to qualify if you are unable to do your own job or a similar one, rather than unable to do *any* job. It should be possible to have a part-pension if you can do a part-time job but not a full-time one.

The decision should be taken by the trustees, on the advice of an independent medical practitioner. The procedure should be open and clear to the member.

All actual and prospective service should be taken into account, and there should be the power to commute the total pension in cases of really serious ill health. Life insurance should be continued during the period up to normal retirement age, at the same level as it was when the member took early retirement.

The scheme should tie in with the company's overall policy on sick pay and sick absence. If people are offered help and advice early on in a period of sickness, and if health and safety issues are properly dealt with, fewer people will need to go through onto the long-term arrangements.

The general arguments for proper ill health provision are that the whole idea of a pension scheme is to protect you and your dependants against the time when you cannot work. Serious ill health is an unforeseeable event similar to death in service, and ought to be treated as such within the pension scheme. Unless there is a decent ill health pension, the family of the person who *doesn't* die in a car crash, but is an invalid for the rest of his or her life, will be much worse off than the family of the person who does die. That is cruel and illogical.

The employer may suggest that the scheme could be abused, or even that people with chronic health conditions will get jobs with the company 'just to take advantage of the pension'. This is absurd. Most companies have medical examinations when people join, and these ought to pick up 'pre-existing' medical conditions. If the trustees foresee difficulties in a particular case, under the Disability Discrimination Act they would be entitled to say – so long as it was justifiable – that a particular individual was not covered for a particular benefit.

Passing the extra cost of setting up a pension early to the individual 'cost centres', rather than paying them from the fund, reduces the chances of managers using ill health retirement as a backdoor way of cutting staff numbers. On the other hand, it could mean that the local managers discourage or obstruct their staff from applying at all, however justified. So monitoring, and a clear published procedure, are vital.

Late retirement

The Government is putting pressure on employers to do more to encourage older workers to stay on. There has been a non-statutory Code of Practice on Age Diversity in Employment since June 1999, and a new European Directive on the subject of age discrimination means that the Government has to produce legislation by 2006 at the latest.[14]

According to the NAPF's survey, 64 per cent of private sector members, and 14 per cent of public sector ones, are in schemes that defer the pension for someone who stays on, with an actuarial increase. They may also have the option of continuing with the pension building up normally. It's not clear from the survey, however, how they select what will be best for the member.

If the pension continues to build up, you will probably also continue to pay contributions like anyone else. (You stop paying NI contributions, however, once you reach state retirement age.) On the other hand, if the pension is frozen and increased by a percentage each year, you normally stop paying contributions.

If you are reducing your hours, or 'downshifting' to a lower-level job after NRD, you will probably be best off with a pension that is frozen and then actuarially increased. If you still expect reasonable pay increases, above the rate of inflation, you would be better off if the pension continued to accrue. Ask what 'actuarial factors' are used for the calculation. In these days of low inflation, they could be higher than the pay increases you expect.

How to tell if you are in a good scheme

A good scheme provides maximum individual choice, both in the ways in which your pension is increased, and in whether you can split the pension and lump sum and take them separately.

The pensions administrator should do the calculations for the individual, and put them in front of him or her to choose, preferably during a one-to-one session where the member can go through everything.

For most schemes, the death benefits should be based on the death-in-service benefits. However, if your scheme has a good pension but a poor death-in-service benefit (explained on pages 87–90), it might be better to say that it should be based on the post-retirement position instead.

Very few people are likely to take up the late retirement option, so cost is really not an issue. For those who do, it will be either because of personal circumstances or because the company is keen to keep them due to their special skills, so they should be given good arrangements.

Lump sum benefits on death in service

According to the NAPF survey, in final-salary schemes 57 per cent of private sector members, but only 2 per cent of public sector members, are covered for the full four times earnings permitted by the IR (see Appendix 1). Nearly 80 per cent of the public sector members are covered for between two and three times salary.[15]

Sometimes different benefits for different groups will be the result of 'red circling' – that is, special provision to ensure that a group with better conditions in one respect do not lose out when the scheme is changed overall. For instance, if a scheme has been changed from giving a death benefit of four times earnings plus a minimal spouse's pension, to one giving two times earnings plus a much better spouse's pension, those who were already members at the time of the change might be allowed to retain the four times earnings. Alternatively, it may be a matter of giving management better value for money in the pension scheme, and so the rest of the workforce subsidizing them.

Some schemes deduct the cost of providing the minimum spouse's pension required for contracting out from the lump sum. This is a penny-pinching measure, which means that the spouse is being asked to pay for his or her own pension, and should be opposed. However, the lump sum and spouse's pension should be looked at together. If there is a good spouse's pension, there is less reason to have a large lump sum as well. So a contracted *in* scheme that does not provide a spouse's pension should give a bigger lump sum than one that does.

Only around a third of members in the private sector, and a tiny proportion in the public sector, are in schemes that give a return of contributions. In some cases this will be instead of the ordinary lump sum, rather than on top of it. However, this is a useful extra benefit to have since it means that the families of the people who have been in the scheme longest will get some direct recompense for all their extra contributions.

How to tell if you are in a good scheme

Roughly speaking, in a scheme which aimed to be a bit better than average you could expect a lump sum of around three times earnings, plus a spouse's pension of half the member's own, based on all prospective service (explained in the next section). In a scheme that aimed to be particularly good, there should be four times earnings plus a two-thirds spouse's pension.

The small print is important. Check:

▋ The definition of earnings. For this purpose, it should be *either* PAYE earnings for the last 12 months, or the last pay period's earnings multiplied up to give an annual figure. If people's

> earnings fluctuate at different times of the year, the first method is better, because otherwise someone dying at the 'wrong' time of year is penalized.
>
> ▌ If someone has been sick for, say, four weeks or more in the final year, a 'notional' PAYE figure should be created. If there's an easily calculated group average, you can use this. Or you could use earnings for the last full year worked, uprated by the increase in prices since that date.
>
> ▌ Interest should be added to the refund of contributions, perhaps at the rate of 4 or 5 per cent.

The arguments for a bigger death benefit are:

▌ it's cost-effective: it takes a comparatively small increase in premiums to give a much better level of benefit;

▌ people feel strongly if someone they have worked with for a long time dies, and the employer treats their dependants shabbily;

▌ the economies of scale are enormous – it's very much cheaper to get insurance for 100 people as a group, than for each of the 100 to go out and buy their own.

The employer's objection will usually be money. However, it is easy to be flexible on this point without damaging or over-complicating the structure of the scheme as a whole.

The employer may also say that they don't feel people will be able to handle a large sum of money, and so it would be wasted. This is a paternalist argument, and also sexist because the implication will be that *wives* and female partners will not be able to handle money. The response is that the employer should ensure that proper financial advice is made available. The employer may say they don't see the need. It could be pointed out that families frequently do have substantial debts, and will have arranged their lives to take account of the flow of income in, so an unexpected death will create considerable problems. Even a young person, not married or with a family, may have piled up debts.

Death benefit is one of the easier things in a pension scheme to change. Even in a large scheme it is usually insured, to safeguard the scheme if a busload of people went over a cliff. So improving it is simply a matter of raising the premium.

You might want to suggest to your union that it keeps an eye on how the benefit is administered. Questions to raise include:

▋ How long is it taking for benefit to be paid out?

▋ Is it simple for members to make their own wishes clear as to where the benefit goes, and to change it when their situation changes – for instance, if they get married or divorced?

▋ Is it genuinely kept confidential? Or, if someone has family circumstances that are not all they seem, are they going to find gossip spreading once they have filled in the nomination form?

Spouses' and dependants' pensions

Only a quarter of schemes pay a pension of two-thirds of the member's own, according to the NAPF, with some paying as little as a fifth. Two-thirds of members are in schemes that take account of prospective as well as actual service. A common pattern is to have a spouse's pension of 50 per cent of the member's own prospective pension, with an additional 25 per cent for each child to a maximum of two children. These figures are then doubled where there are dependent children but no spouse.

Many schemes, including those in the public sector, will only pay the pension to the legally married spouse, not a common-law partner. This was the case throughout the public services until recently, but the new Civil Service scheme does allow for dependants' benefits. Many other scheme rules require a nomination – not necessarily in writing – before the trustees will consider granting a pension to a non-relative.

The rules may say that an adult dependant's pension will only be paid where there was no spouse, or they may allow for the pension itself to be divided. In a contracted out scheme, the legal widow/er must receive the GMP or the pension derived from the protected rights, whatever happens to the rest.

How to tell if you are in a good scheme

A good scheme will offer maximum flexibility, including pensions for non-married partners of either sex. This is not expensive, since the actuary will already have needed to calculate the scheme's costs on the assumption that most people are married.

It is reasonable for the trustees to ask for a nomination, or proof from the potential beneficiary, that they were dependent on the member, as this will avoid the scheme being taken for a ride by someone who might only have had a casual relationship.

Some schemes reduce the amount of pension where the spouse is more than, say, 10 years younger than the member, and/or end the pension if the spouse remarries (or lives with someone as husband and wife). Rules like this are penny-pinching and insulting, and should be abolished. In some cases where this has been done – for instance with British Telecom – widow/ers who had lost their pensions under a remarriage rule had them reinstated when the rule was abolished. This is unlikely to cost much, but will create a lot of goodwill.

Some schemes provide a widower's pension based only on service since 1988 (when the Equal Treatment rules, explained on page 22, came in). The local government scheme, for example, did this until recently. It has now swept this restriction away, and other schemes ought to follow suit. It is cheap to provide full widowers' benefits, since most women outlive their husbands.

Children's pensions

All public sector members, and nearly 90 per cent of private sector members, are in schemes that provide children's benefits on top of the spouse's pension. A few private sector schemes provide them only for orphan children (where the member and the spouse have both died), or only at the trustees' discretion.[16]

Having children's pensions is not expensive, since most of those who die in service will be older and no longer have dependent children. The aim should be to get the maximum the IR will allow, with a doubling of benefit not only for orphan children but also for those of single parents generally.

Arguments to use are: first, that since a contracted out scheme must pay some spouses' benefits, it ought to provide good ones. A small pension for a spouse may simply deprive him or her of the ability to claim means-tested benefits. Second, extending the pension to dependants other than spouses improves the position particularly for non-married partners, or people in same-sex relationships. It would also give a pension to the member's elderly parent, or a brother or sister who has been unable to earn his or her own living. Now that even the Civil Service has accepted this in its new scheme, it is hard for anyone to argue against it.

Death after retirement

Most schemes provide a spouse's pension for death after retirement. Many also have rules allowing 'surrender' of part of the member's pension to increase that for the spouse, but these are very rarely used. Most schemes will have a half-pension for the spouse, but those that provide two-thirds for death in service may also do so for death after retirement.

Most schemes have a five-year guarantee for the pension. This is really a reassurance that all members will receive a minimum value for money. If the member dies before five years' payments of pension have been made, the balance of those five years' money is paid as a lump sum to their estate, or as a continuing pension to the spouse. So, for instance, if a member were to die after only 18 months' pension had been paid, another three years and six months' worth would be due.

Some schemes only pay the 'balance' if there is no spouse to get a continuing pension. Others 'discount' (reduce) the future pension payments when they calculate them, on the artificial assumption that the person receiving the payment will invest the lump sum and add back the interest payments. The best arrangement is for the scheme to pay out the total amount that would have been due (apart from discretionary increases that have not yet been decided on).

Very few schemes provide a bereavement benefit, or the extra life cover the IR allows, because it creates problems for scheme administrators in checking whether you are within the IR limits. The exception is where someone has retired early due to ill health, where some schemes do continue life cover up until retirement age. This is very well worthwhile, as the member may find it impossible to get life insurance any other way.

How to tell if you are in a good scheme

Most schemes provide a 50 per cent spouse's pension, but some of the better ones will pay two-thirds. A good scheme extends the pension to other adult dependants, and has a good five-year guarantee.

The scheme ought not to have rules saying that the pension stops if the spouse remarries or lives with someone as husband and wife. Such rules really are distasteful when you are talking about elderly pensioners, as are rules limiting the pension for 'deathbed marriages'. Under these, the scheme may say that if the member marries after retirement and dies within six months, only the spouses' GMP will be paid.

You could suggest to your union that they try to have any improvement backdated to cover existing pensioners and their spouses or dependants as well (so far as the IR limits allow). The cost is unlikely to be very large.

In general, the death-in-service and death-after-retirement benefits run in parallel with each other. A breakthrough on one will usually be followed by a breakthrough on the other.

Pension increases

In public sector pension schemes (and some of the schemes in the former nationalized industries), increases in line with the RPI are *guaranteed*. This may not seem very important at present, with inflation so low, but if we ever go back to the sort of price rises we were seeing in the 1970s and 1980s, those pensioners will be the lucky ones.

In the private sector, according to the NAPF, for post-1997 pensions around a quarter of members are in schemes that give guaranteed increases on a better level than LPI. Generally, this will mean that they will not impose the 5 per cent ceiling if inflation goes above that level. The rest give guarantees that do as well, or in some cases better than LPI and then review every so often to see if the pension fund is healthy enough to allow an increase.

Though there's no legal requirement to index extra pre-1997 benefits above GMP, in practice most schemes do so, at least to some extent – often at the trustees' discretion.

A few schemes, such as Legal and General's one for its staff, give guaranteed increases of a fixed percentage; in L&G's case 3 per cent a year, regardless of what happens to inflation.[17]

How to tell if you are in a good scheme

In the better schemes, instead of having pension increases paid 'at the discretion' of the trustees – or sometimes the company – they are guaranteed to be paid as of right. It is not easy to achieve this, though, as companies will be frightened of the cost.

Another issue is past increases for pensioners, especially those who retired when inflation was much higher and saw their

> pensions cut away in real value very quickly. If there is a surplus
> in the scheme (explained on page 144) they should really have
> first call on this. However, even if the company wants to do some-
> thing on this, the new standard for company accounts (FRS17,
> explained on page 183) will mean that the cost will show up
> painfully in the books.

There is a pensioners lobby in the public sector, and some good
private sector schemes, for pensions-in-payment to be linked to
earnings increases rather than prices. This is perfectly logical, since
only linking with price increases means one's standard of living
falls behind the rest of the world's. Unfortunately, it is pie in the sky,
as, given the cost, no government is going to concede it to people
who can't go on strike.

Early leavers

The law on this was explained in Chapter 5. The core public service
schemes are the best for their treatment of early leavers. They:

I   revalue their deferred pensions in line with the rise in the RPI;

I   cover a whole occupation, rather than an individual employer.
    No matter how often a teacher moves between schools or
    education authorities, for example, he or she can stay a member
    of the single national Teachers' Pension Scheme; and

I   have formed a 'transfer club'. In general, if you move from one
    of these schemes to another – say, local government to the Civil
    Service – and start to transfer your pension within a certain
    time limit, it will be done on a favourable basis. This may be
    'year-on-year', that is, a year in the old one will count as a year
    in the new. Where there are differences between the schemes,
    such as a difference in retirement age, there will be an adjust-
    ment to take account of this. Where there is a longer time lag,
    the favourable rates do not apply, but the government actuary
    draws up tables showing what value will be given.

In the private sector, most schemes only do what they legally have
to. Three-quarters of private sector members are in schemes that
give the statutory increases only, with the rest giving some additional discretionary increases, or a guaranteed level of increase.

Transfer values are more standardized than they used to be, because of the legal requirements. However, many schemes refuse to take transfers-*in*. This is partly because of fears that they might have to meet Equal Treatment claims for the money that is brought over. It is also convenient for schemes, though, because it means that they avoid extra administration and do not need to worry about what values they use for those leaving. Many also do not include 'discretionary' early retirement options when calculating the pension, as explained on page 80.

How to tell if you are in a good scheme

The ideal is for all deferred pensions to be increased in line with the RPI, without a ceiling. Another possibility, rather less good, is that the rules say that if the trustees give the pensioners discretionary increases, the deferred pensions will be increased by the same amount. Transfer values should anyway include discretionary increases.

Another option is the 'belt and braces' approach of turning your scheme into a *hybrid* scheme (explained on page 17) with a money-purchase underpin. This would mean that if the investment returns on an individual's contributions, plus at least part of the employer's contribution, gave a better result than the final-salary formula and LPI increases, then that is what you would get. This does, however, make the scheme more expensive, not surprisingly, and it makes it much less likely that there will be a surplus (explained in Chapter 9).

Advice to leavers

Knowing when to leave your pension with the scheme and when to take a transfer, and where to transfer to, can be a minefield. Some good employers, such as Sainsbury's, make help available to their staff on this. Sainsbury's has a contract with a reputable firm of financial advisers who run a 'transfer desk'. They can give advice and arrange a deal with an insurance company if that is suitable. This does not come cheap for the employer, but would be a benefit well worth having. If you cannot obtain it as a regular feature, try at least to get help if there is a group leaving because of a redundancy package or a closure.

Death while a pension is being deferred

In general, once the member has left the scheme the lump sum death benefit disappears, and the spouses' pension may well go down to the minimum. Especially if people are leaving through no fault of their own – for instance due to a redundancy – the employer may be willing to arrange for the life assurance to continue to cover them for up to six months. Alternatively, people may be allowed to continue the life assurance at their own cost, but with a special concession such as no medical evidence being required.

According to the NAPF, around 7 per cent of private sector schemes – presumably all contracted in – gave nothing at all on death in deferment, and another 6 per cent only gave the minimum pension to meet the contracting out requirements. The majority gave a pension, which would generally be 50 per cent of the member's own deferred pension, and some also gave a refund of the member's contributions.

It is difficult for unions to negotiate improvements in this aspect alone, partly because members are not very interested in the people who have already left. However, improvements in the benefits for death in service and in retirement ought also to be followed through for death in deferment. It is important to have it spelt out clearly in the scheme booklet what the position is, as this could be a major factor for anyone deciding whether or not to transfer his or her deferred pension elsewhere.

Paying for improvements

When the unions are making a claim for pension improvements, they would generally want to compile a 'shopping list' that includes a mixture of high- and low-cost items. Some examples of high-cost items, costing perhaps 3–4 per cent of payroll, are:

- improving the accrual rate substantially;

- providing for past service at a reasonable rate;

- reducing the retirement age, or the age at which people can take early retirement as of right, by several years;

- removing the integration factor;

- providing for automatic increases in pensions, beyond the legal minimum.

Small improvements in these items would cost much less. Reducing the retirement age by only one year, for instance, would be a moderate cost item.

Moderately expensive items, somewhere between 1 and 2 per cent of payroll, might include:

▌ improving the spouse's pension from an accrued to a prospective basis;

▌ giving a better deal for early retirement at the employer's or member's request, such as cutting the percentage reduction for each year someone is going early;

▌ improving the ill health provision if it is currently very limited, or creating a PHI scheme;

▌ giving an extra year's earnings in the lump sum death benefit.

Cheaper improvements, costing less than 1 per cent of payroll, would include:

▌ giving pensions to non-married partners;

▌ giving or improving dependent children's pensions;

▌ improving the definition of pensionable or final pensionable earnings;

▌ improving temporary absence provisions;

▌ improving the commutation rate.

Extending the scheme to new groups of people costs money on a different basis. It brings more people on to the pensionable payroll, so that the employer has to find an extra contribution for each one.

It is useful also to divide the items into those that stand by themselves, and those that have a 'knock-on' effect, because they improve not only the pension but also the early retirement benefit, the spouse's pension and the life assurance. Those that 'knock-on' are:

▌ providing for past service;

▌ improving the accrual rate;

▌ removing the integration factor;

▌ improving the earnings or final earnings definition.

It is possible to work out roughly how much an improvement will cost by seeing what the effect on the average pension will be, and then thinking how many people will be affected. For example, going from a 1/80th rate to a 1/60th one will give everyone one-third more in pension – so you can assume the scheme will cost that much more for future service. If you are trying to increase it for past service as well, the cost will be considerably more as the employer will need to pay the extra money over a fairly short time. The way that pensions are treated now in company accounts (under the FRS17 rules, explained in the Glossary) makes it rather difficult to achieve a backdated increase of this sort.

Costs are generally given as a percentage of payroll. You should be able to find out the current total payroll cost for your employer from their annual accounts. The *pensionable* payroll figure may be different (because not all pay is pensionable). A breakdown of the figures for different groups of benefits should be in the latest actuarial valuation, though if it is a year or two old you may need to do your own calculations to bring the figures up to date.

Surpluses

Over most of the 1980s and 1990s, many salary-related pension schemes built up big surpluses in their funds, which made it fairly easy for the unions to negotiate improvements. No extra money was needed to come in from either employer or employee to pay for the improvements, for several years or perhaps for the foreseeable future.

However, surpluses are now disappearing. Low inflation and investment returns, coupled with legal requirements for increases in pensions and deferred pensions (explained in Chapter 5) mean that employers are now having to pay the real costs of the benefit package they have set up, perhaps for the first time ever. It's one reason that so many final-salary schemes are now being closed to new entrants.

If you are lucky enough to have a surplus in the scheme at the next actuarial valuation, you and your fellow scheme members will want to press the union to discuss with the employer what to do with it. The starting point is usually to say that as the pension is the members' deferred pay, it should all be used for their benefit. Sadly, this is not very realistic, and we have to expect that the employer will want to reap *some* benefit from it.

One major reason for actuarial surpluses has been that pensioners and deferred pensioners have had very small increases in the past, while the money set aside to cover their benefits has been earning interest at a much higher rate. So logically and morally, they should have first call on any surplus. Their benefits should be increased up to the rise in the RPI since the last increase was given. In some cases, the trustees may have the powers to do this themselves, but more often the company will have a power of veto. It should, therefore, be a matter of negotiation.

The employer may be wary of offering improvements that have a permanent cost effect, if the surplus is only temporary. Many employers have been willing, though, to use surpluses for improving the early retirement package for a fixed period, at a time when they want to reduce staff anyway. Ideally, this should be traded off against something else on the 'shopping list'.

Contribution holidays or surplus payments

If there is a surplus, the company can take a payment directly out of the fund. This is taxed at 35 per cent, however, so it is not a very efficient use of the money. The employer also has to go through a very long procedure (more or less the same as that explained on page 144, for taking a surplus when the scheme winds up) before being allowed to do so. It is bound to be controversial with the members, as for example the Thorn Pension Fund trustees found when they began the process to pay £80m to the employer. Companies that want to duck this sort of controversy would prefer to take a contribution holiday, even if it takes rather longer for them to have the full benefit of the money.

It is tempting to ask for the members to have a contribution holiday also, but it is usually a mistake. It carries the disadvantages of a non-contributory scheme, explained on page 64. The members will lose interest, and control. You also create a very difficult situation when the holiday ends. All of a sudden, the members have to start paying again. This could eat up much of a pay rise for that year. It is best if members put the same amount of contributions into their AVCs (explained in Chapter 10) so that they still have the money taken out of their pay packet.

If the employer is determined to have a contribution holiday, rather than make improvements, there is little members or their unions can do to stop it. There have been a whole series of court cases trying to establish rights for members to have a share of the surplus, going right up to the House of Lords. The most they have been able to establish is that members have a right to be *considered* for use of the surplus, but the trustees are allowed to take the employer's interest into account; and employers must act properly and in good faith: there is a limit to how far they can go in effectively asset-stripping a pension fund.

The rule of thumb that has been established is that around a two-thirds/one-third division is not unreasonable. It is always worth fighting for more, though, checking carefully on the legal position and using the publicity weapon where one can.

Actuarial deficits

These seem likely to become far more common in the future than they have in the recent past. They arise when there is not enough money forecast to go into the scheme to meet the benefits promised. If the trustees are convinced that the money will not be forthcoming, they must reduce the benefits or close down the scheme, but that is a last resort. Before that, they should make every effort to get the employer to make up the necessary contributions. Sorting out a deficit has to be the first priority, before looking for improvements.

Notes

1. Table 16.
2. Taken from *Pension Scheme Profiles 2001/2*, Incomes Data Services 2001 p 56.
3. *Pension Scheme Profiles*, p 56.
4. 'Pensioners enjoy full inflation-proofing', *Occupational Pensions*, December 2001, p 13.
5. Taken from their booklet, p 7.
6. Both examples taken from *Pension Scheme Profiles*.
7. Taken from their scheme booklet, dated October 1999.
8. 'Commuting pensions', *IDS Pensions Bulletin 149*, October 2001, pp 4–6.
9. 'Are retirees sensible to commute their pension?', *Pensions*, PricewaterhouseCoopers, August/September 2001.
10. NAPF 2001 survey, table 34.
11. Table 43.
12. Table 44.
13. Case J00466, reported in *Annual Report of the Pensions Ombudsman*, 2000–1, p 23, London, 2001.
14. Minutes of Evidence 14 June 2001, response to question 33, House of Commons Employment Committee.
15. Tables 53 and 54.
16. Table 48.
17. Ditto, p 210.

9 *What makes a good money-purchase scheme?*

Occupational or personal/stakeholder?

Questions you need to ask:

- █ What sort of scheme is it – occupational or personal/stakeholder?
- █ Why has this sort of pension been chosen and not one of the other varieties?
- █ Can anyone who wants to join?
- █ How much do I have to pay in, and how much does the employer pay?
- █ If I have already got a pension with someone else, will the employer pay contributions into that scheme instead?
- █ What happens if I want to change my contributions?
- █ Is all my pay pensionable?
- █ What charges does the insurance company (or other provider) make, and who carries these – the employer or me? What effect will they have on my pension?
- █ If the scheme is not a stakeholder scheme, are the charges different from those that would be charged if it were a stakeholder? In what way? Why has the employer chosen this scheme rather than a stakeholder?
- █ What choice of funds do I have?
- █ What if I want to retire early?
- █ What if I fall ill and can no longer work?
- █ What happens at retirement? Is there an open market option for the annuity?
- █ What benefits are there if I die?
- █ What happens if I leave the employer? Is there a change in the charges?

A money-purchase scheme can either be occupational (looked after by trustees on behalf of the group as a whole), or personal (with each individual buying a policy from an insurance company or other provider). Most stakeholder schemes are run by insurance companies in the same way as other personal pensions, but there are some – including the one sponsored by the TUC – which have trustees, though you still buy an individual policy.

The right choice depends very much on the size and security of the company, and how much trouble it is willing to put into the scheme. The trustees of a large occupational scheme can afford to buy in the best investment experts and professional advisers, and keep up to date with changes in the law and in the world around them, in a way that individuals cannot expect to. They are also in a position to beat down the fees that the investment managers and insurance companies are charging, and ensure that the members receive a good package of benefits.

However, in a smaller company the trustees may not have much more knowledge than anyone else, or the resources or the willpower to buy in the expertise. They may then be at the mercy of the insurance company or financial adviser who sold them the scheme. In a company that has cash-flow problems or is badly managed, there may be a danger that contributions do not flow into the scheme as they should and that record keeping is neglected. This would affect a personal/stakeholder scheme as well, but at least in those cases the individual would have control over his or her own 'pension pot'. So in these circumstances you might want to concentrate on obtaining the maximum contribution from the employer into the employees' pensions, but not try to get them involved in the running of it.

A personal/stakeholder pension could also be the best option where staff are on short-term contracts, or the employment itself is not going to last very long. Something like a quarter of Sainsbury's staff are now students, for example, so having a stakeholder scheme they can take with them makes sense. These schemes can also cater for periods when one is self-employed or unemployed, while occupational schemes cannot.

So it should be 'horses for courses' – think of what is on offer, and what is within the employer's competence, as well as what you might ideally want.

Who should be able to join?

There are no statistics about who is being allowed to join GPP or stakeholder schemes set up by the employer. At a guess, however, this happens where the employer has designed a GPP specifically for the workforce, and is putting in a substantial contribution. There may be restrictions similar to those in occupational schemes, with a bare-bones stakeholder scheme alongside. It also happens where it is a lower-standard GPP or stakeholder, set up to meet the legal requirements; the restrictions will probably mirror those laid down in the regulations. In particular, the rules may say that people must have worked for the employer for at least three months, earning over the Lower Earnings Limit. Some GPPs, however, are very inclusive, often because of the special circumstances of their industry.

At the BBC, as well as its long-standing final-salary scheme there is a GPP that is available to long- and short-term employees, contractors and self-employed people carrying out work for the corporation. It has recognized that the workforce in the television industry is a very fluid one, and people may do a series of different pieces of work for the BBC over long periods of time, while working for other people in the meantime.

As with a final-salary pension scheme (see page 60) the aim should be to have as few restrictions as possible. If the charges are on the stakeholder basis, then however short a time the individual stays with the firm, he or she will be able to benefit from the pension, because it can be picked up and taken elsewhere.

There is more of a problem if people arrive with a personal pension already, from another employer or one they have set up themselves. If it is an older PP, stopping contributions may mean meeting extra charges, but carrying on with the PP may mean fore-going the employer's contribution. Ideally, employers should be willing to pay into more than one provider's scheme, but the insurance companies' systems are so cumbersome that this is making more work than most employers would want to take on. Since most people are not paying anything like the maximum they could into a personal/stakeholder pension, in many cases it will be possible for people to have two pensions running at the same time – one into which they are paying in, one for the employer's contributions.

Gaps in employment

The law on this was explained in Chapter 8. With a stakeholder scheme, there must be no extra charges for stopping or starting contributions, or for reducing them. With a GPP, though, there may be, and the employer should be pressed to renegotiate these with the provider.

If the employer is making deductions from employees' pay packets to go into the pension, they are entitled to say that they will only allow the amount to be changed every six months. Press them to be more flexible, at least in situations that are covered by other negotiated agreements. Again, press for any life insurance benefit (and PHI, if possible) to be continued during a period of absence. The arguments will be the same as suggested above for occupational schemes.

The key issue: contributions

The major focus needs to be on pushing up the level of employers' contributions. There is much evidence that employers are using the move to money-purchase as a way of cutting their costs. The NAPF survey, for example, shows an average employer contribution of 6.4 per cent, compared to 8.3 per cent for a final-salary scheme. Another survey, of over 400 firms employing fewer than 250 people, found that combined employer and employee contributions into money-purchase schemes averaged under 9 per cent of earnings, some 5–7 per cent below those in final-salary schemes. Many employers with stakeholder schemes are putting in no contribution whatsoever.

How much do you need?

To buy a good money-purchase pension, equivalent to a good final-salary pension, probably more than the employer will give you!

Pension costs have risen in recent years, so what might have been adequate in the past is no longer so.

One study took a man who was 30 in 1986, paying 10 per cent into a money-purchase scheme. It then looked at what each year's projected figure would have told him, taking account of the investment performance of the fund already built up. At the beginning, this person might have been told by the actuary that he could look forward to a pension of 56 per cent of his expected final earnings. By now, the same person's projected pension, with investment returns falling and life expectancy going up, would be 35 per cent.

Often when the employer is moving from a final-salary to a money-purchase scheme, or has done so in the past, they may have suggested that 'we are not doing this for cost-cutting reasons'. That's not usually true, but statements like that give you leverage if you can show that the employer's costs have gone down.

A recent calculation by one of the actuarial organizations asked the question, 'What do I need to save in pension contributions to achieve a pension of 60 per cent of earnings at age 65?' The answer is shown in Table 9.1.

Table 9.1 Contributions needed to achieve a pension of 60 per cent of earnings at age 65

Age commencing pension	Guideline contribution as per cent of earnings payble until age 65*
Age 25	10–15%
Age 30	12–17%
Age 35	15–20%
Age 40	17–24%
Age 45	23–30%
Age 50	32–45%
Age 55	50–70%

*Assumptions: investment growth of 4 per cent in excess of RPI; annuity based on investment return of 2.5 per cent over pension increases; 1.5 per cent salary increases over RPI; on retirement, inflation linked annuity purchased with a 50 per cent spouse's pension; 1 per cent charges on fund; no previous pension savings; contracted in to SERPS

Source: Association of Consulting Actuaries, 2001

How to tell if you are in a good scheme

A total contribution of 15 per cent is probably the minimum needed to ensure a decent pension – or more if possible. The employer should be paying at least two-thirds of the total contribution – say, 10 per cent to the employee's 5 per cent, in a scheme with 15 per cent going in altogether. Make sure you are clear about whether these figures include, or are on top of, the NI rebate for employers (explained on page 38). It can make a big difference.

The employer should pay for the 'insurance benefits' (death-in-service and disability benefits) separately, and not link them directly with the scheme. That way, more can be paid overall, and the employer should be able to reduce costs by using its 'bulk-buying' power.

The structure of contributions

Employers may argue for increased levels of contribution for more senior staff (especially those in managerial grades), or those who have been there longest. Other, rather better possibilities are matching the contribution the employee makes, either by the same percentage or a higher percentage (perhaps 2 per cent for every 1 per cent, up to a ceiling), or increasing contributions by age.

The argument for matching is that it gives people an incentive to join, and to pay in as much as they can afford. With stakeholder pensions, the evidence is that if the employer simply sets up the scheme and is offering no contribution, perhaps 10 per cent of the workforce join. If the employer *is* making a contribution, up to 90 per cent join. It is really common sense – not to join means handing back money the employer is offering, and who would want to do that?

However, the matching rules should not be too rigid, so that those who can only afford to put in a little still receive some help from the employer. In the Legal and General GPP, for example, the employer puts in 2 per cent even if the employee pays nothing, and will match their contribution up to a maximum of 5 per cent.

Increasing contributions by age – in the same way as the NI rebate is increased – is useful because of the way any money-purchase scheme works. The older you are, the shorter the time left for investment returns and interest payments to build up.

An example

Eddie is 20 and Annie is 40. Each of them puts in a single £1,000 contribution into their pension scheme at the beginning. This increases by 7 per cent compound each year, until they both retire at 60.

Age	Eddie £	Annie £
20	1,000	
30	2,000	
40	4,000	1,000
50	8,000	2,000
60	16,000	4,000

If Annie wants the same amount of pension from her contribution at 40 as Eddie will have from his at 20, she would need to put in £4,000 to start with.

We have used 7 per cent in this example because as it happens, with compound interest at 7 per cent an investment doubles in money value over 10 years. If the interest rate were higher, the gap between the two would be much larger.

Bank of America has a non-contributory money-purchase scheme. The company puts in 6 per cent for those aged between 25 and 29, 9 per cent for those aged between 30 and 39, and 12 per cent for those aged 40 and over.

Pensionable earnings

All pay should be considered as pensionable, so that whatever contribution you have persuaded the employer to make is based on the highest possible pay figure. In a good occupational scheme, with good investment returns, this could mean that the occasional person hits the IR limits on the benefits he or she can take from the scheme at retirement (explained in Appendix 1). It would be better to make it clear in the booklet that this might happen, however, than to depress the pay formula for everyone on the off-chance that it might.

Charges

In a good occupational scheme, the employer will pay the costs of running it and the investment costs. In a poorer scheme, however, and in many GPPs and stakeholder schemes, it is the individual who will pay the costs.

If the scheme is described as a stakeholder, the charges cannot be more than 1 per cent of the fund per year, with no penalties for starting or stopping contributions or for taking your money elsewhere. If it is described as anything else, however – and there are some products using weasel words such as 'stakeholder friendly' – you have no such guarantee.

One of the most confusing elements is the 'allocation rate'. Advertisements claiming '102 per cent allocation' or '105 per cent allocation' merely mean that the value of contributions is grossed up to that level before deductions are taken from it; no extra money is going into the member's account.

With the advent of stakeholder schemes, the insurance companies have had to reduce and simplify their charges considerably.

However, if the policy was taken out some time ago, the charges may not have been reviewed and reduced, but remain as they were under the old contract. If an independent financial adviser (IFA) is receiving a regular payment of commission for this, they may be reluctant to push for change.

Even with new contracts, some GPP charges are a great deal higher than others. They vary in the way they deduct money, so that some will be better for higher earners making large contributions over a long period, others for people making smaller contributions or over a shorter time. If you can only afford to put in £50 a month, you don't want a policy that charges you a flat-rate fee while benefiting the person who puts in £500 a month.

If any money-purchase pension – no matter what it is called – is deducting more than 1 per cent in charges from anyone, you will want to know the reason. It would need to be a pretty good one for the scheme to be value for money. The Financial Services Authority Web site (www.fsa.gov.uk) gives details of the charges of all the personal pension providers (except a couple which will not cooperate with them). Charges are not everything, though: you have to look at performance as well, and at what extras are being offered for the additional cost.

Investment arrangements

Giving scheme members a choice of funds to invest in is quite usual. This can allow people to put their money in all the major investment categories: equities, bonds and property, and variations such as index-linked securities and international equities. Usually, some of the funds on offer will be higher-risk than others, and this should be spelt out in the publicity material. Many schemes, however, do not offer any choice to their members.

According to one recent survey, around 25 per cent of schemes do not give their members a choice of different funds, though 50 per cent offered five funds or more. Eighty-five per cent had a 'default' arrangement, that is a fund into which people were automatically put if they did not make the choice themselves. However, the survey quoted above suggests that around a third of default funds were not suitable for their purpose. Most schemes have a 'lifestyle' arrangement. Share prices go up and down with the stock market, and this makes it difficult for those coming up to retirement to plan their future. 'Lifestyling' means that the fund account is moved gradually, over perhaps five or 10 years as the members approach retirement, into a gilts fund, which is likely to have steadier (though perhaps lower) returns. GUS plc, for example, explains that for those who have gone with the trustees' choice of investments:

In the five years up to your 'Target Retirement Date' your individual account will gradually be switched out of the M&G UK Equity Fund into Units in the M&G Index Linked Gilt and Cash fund so that, by your Target Retirement Date, all your individual account will be invested in these funds.

Lifestyling can be very inflexible, however, making no allowance for people's wishes to take early retirement. As one expert from the US (where lifestyling has not taken off) has commented, 'I have never seen two 55-year-olds who are the same.'

Another alternative is 'tracker' funds, which are invested in all or a reasonable sample of the shares within a particular index. They will not outperform it, but nor will they grossly underperform either.

How to tell if you are in a good scheme

If lifestyling is used, it should be flexible, allowing individuals to select the date at which they aim to retire, and change it if circumstances alter.

Every stakeholder scheme must have a 'default' arrangement – a fund into which contributions go if the member selects nothing else. This is a rather lazy British way of doing things. In the United States, the trustees or providers have to offer investment education to the members, and employers should be pressed to follow this example. In any case, the default fund needs to be monitored by the trustees or an advisory committee to ensure it remains suitable, and the options available should be explained clearly to the members.

Choosing the provider

It's up to the employer or trustees they choose to provide the arrangement into which they will pay contributions. Any individual is free to go elsewhere, of course, but if the employer will only pay contributions into one specific scheme, this might be cutting off your nose to spite your face.

Where an employer is designating a stakeholder scheme, as explained in Chapter 3, the unions and members must be consulted. 'Consultation', though, is not defined in the regulations. Opra's guide for employers suggests that they might:

▌ already have a discussion process in place;

▌ give details about possible stakeholder pension schemes to employees at a meeting; or

▌ give the employees written details and ask for their views.

This is a very limited view of consultation, however. The key question is really whether the employer is willing to change its mind after the exercise, or whether it is just cosmetic. Will you have the chance, for instance, to explain why you prefer the TUC stakeholder scheme to the one the employer has chosen, and hear the employer's reasons for rejecting it? If the employer is using an IFA or consultant to set up the scheme – as would be usual with a firm of any size – you should ask the unions to ensure that they are included in the discussions on the selection process.

Benefits, early retirement and ill health

Occupational schemes follow the same IR rules for early retirement as final-salary schemes, explained in Appendix 1. Personal/stakeholder schemes must allow you to start drawing your pension at any age from 50 onwards, but the Protected Rights fund in a pension that has been contracted out of SERPS/S2P cannot be paid before you are 60. So if only the NI rebate, or a little more, has gone into your policy, there will be little or nothing to draw on anyway.

There is usually a retirement age built into the contract, and you will be penalized (in terms of the amount of pension you get) for retiring any earlier. However, if you choose to start taking the pension regardless, the employer cannot prevent you, and you are entitled to draw the pension and continue working at the same time.

Generally, money-purchase schemes are not good at providing for early retirement. You have your own account, the 'pot' of money with your name on. If you are retiring early, the pot will be smaller to start with, and will buy a great deal less at, say, 55 than it will at 65. Unless the employer adds something – in fact, quite a lot – to the pot, people will probably not be able to afford to retire. Very few employers are willing to put in extra money at this stage, and they may well not be able to afford to do so at the time when it is needed. One exception is at Norwich Union, where a single employer contribution will be provided, in the event of redundancy, for members aged 50 and above. This will be 2 per cent of pensionable salary for each year of service, to a maximum of 24 per cent of salary.

The fallback is to have as good a redundancy pay package as possible, and for people to have the option to put some of it into the pension scheme. It might then be better if the bulk of the redundancies come from younger people, who are still in a position to get good jobs elsewhere and build up their benefits, rather than people old enough to take early retirement.

Permanent health insurance

If you have to go due to ill health, the early retirement pension will simply be the annuity bought with the value of the accumulated fund, as if you were going of your own accord. In a personal/stakeholder scheme, the insurance company will take the decision on whether one qualifies since there are generally no trustees. For this reason many schemes have a separately insured disability benefit or permanent health insurance, providing a benefit that is a proportion of earnings. This is sometimes known instead as 'disability insurance' or 'income protection insurance'.

PHI is designed to pick up where the employer's sick pay scheme leaves off, and to pay a benefit for as long as the individual is incapacitated. It is usually calculated as a gross figure of between 50 and 75 per cent of usual earnings from work, with the state incapacity benefit and other benefits offset against it. Some policies offer benefit on a 'net pay' basis, taking account of the individual's tax position. In addition, the PHI usually pays the individual's pension contribution, so that at scheme retirement date they will normally move on to the occupational pension.

Often there are exclusions from the policy, such as pregnancy-related illnesses and AIDS-related diseases. Employers do not always read the small print and understand exactly what is covered, before signing up for a PHI policy, or notice what changes are made in future years. If there is a clash between the policy wording and the contract of employment or what has been announced to the workforce, the employer may well be bound by the contract or announcement. You may need to get legal advice on this, however, or to go to the Financial Ombudsman Service (address in Appendix 4). Ask your union for help, or go to a law centre or Citizens Advice Bureau if necessary.

The 'permanent' refers to the fact that once the benefit is in payment and the individual remains incapacitated, it is not stopped even if the employer stops paying the premium. The insurers can still raise the premiums, or decline further business from employers where the health record is bad. In recent years a number have asked for massive premium increases, or closed their books to new clients.

Normally PHI is non-contributory for the employee, and the employer's contributions are treated as a business expense. It is covered by European Union laws on equal treatment of men and women, so that the same amount must be paid under the same conditions. Women are, however, considerably more expensive to cover for PHI than men, because insurance company statistics show them as having a worse sickness record. The sickness figures for manual workers are also much higher than for white-collar workers, which makes it more expensive to insure them.

How to tell if you are in a good scheme

A good PHI scheme has a good level of benefit – two-thirds of earnings if possible. If state benefits are taken into account, this should be only the individual's benefits, not anything for his or her family.

It should be arranged so that it is not caught by the new 'offsetting' arrangements in state Incapacity Benefit, explained on page 9. Currently, PHI arrangements where employees contribute part of the cost are not common, but they may become so in future. Existing employees should be given a one-off increase to cover the cost of any new deduction from pay. Otherwise, they will be taking a pay-cut.

Other things to look for are:

▌ regular annual increases, and continued payment of pension contributions;

▌ covering everyone, from the time they join the company if possible;

▌ as few exclusions as possible – look particularly at AIDS-related illnesses, and 'sports' or 'self-inflicted' injuries (which can penalize people who go skiing);

▌ tying in with the sickness scheme; if sick-pay runs for only 6 months, the PHI should kick in after that.

PHI arrangements also need monitoring. If the insurer appears to be rejecting justified claims, you and your fellow members may want to press the company and the unions to intervene. This may involve helping individuals through the insurance company's complaints process and if necessary up to the Financial Ombudsman Service. It may be possible to change insurer but, particularly if the policy has been running for some time, the company could find that the premiums increase sharply by doing so.

What happens at retirement

Cash lump sum

For an occupational scheme, the rules about what you can take as cash, and how it is worked out, are the same as for a final-salary scheme, explained on page 77. The same issues arise, so look at Chapter 8 to find out more.

For a personal/stakeholder scheme, you are allowed to take up to 25 per cent of the fund in cash. However, if you have been contracted out of SERPS/S2P, you cannot take any of your Protected Rights fund (explained on page 39) as cash – it must be turned into pension. So if only the NI rebate has been going into the pension policy there will be no 'free money' available as cash. If there have been extra contributions above the rebate from you or your employer, there will be some free money.

Buying the pension

The pool of money left, after taking the cash lump sum, will be used to buy you an 'annuity'. Larger occupational schemes may provide this themselves, while the smaller schemes and GPP/stakeholder schemes will set them up with an insurance company.

GPP/stakeholder schemes *must*, and occupational schemes *may*, allow the member to shop around for the best annuity rate available, and this is called the 'open market option' (OMO). This is important, as annuity rates can vary considerably between different insurers. There are specialist advisers who can help find the best rate at any one time. They can also advise on the many different types of annuity available (see the address list in Appendix 4).

Income drawdown

This is explained on page 171. The IR and the Financial Services Authority (FSA; see page 178 for an explanation of who they are) have imposed some tight limits on this. You must take regular advice to ensure you are not drawing down too much from the fund. This means that it is not sensible to think of income draw-down unless you have a personal pension fund of at least £100,000, plus other income. If you are relying solely on the pension fund, the figure is more like £250,000.

Spouses and dependants

For personal/stakeholder schemes, the member has to choose at retirement whether to buy a spouse's or dependant's annuity, so that money continues to be paid after he or she dies (see page 37 for the contracting out position). This annuity must not be larger than the member's own. If the member is doing 'income draw-down', the position is complex, and anyone thinking of this needs to ensure they understand the implications for their spouse, before they start the process.

How to tell if you are in a good scheme

Unless the scheme is subsidizing the annuity rate, there should be an OMO for annuity purchase, with advice available to members.

Some insurers penalize those who move their money else-where at retirement, or offer a loyalty bonus to those who stay (which comes to much the same thing). They should be avoided when setting up a new scheme.

Income drawdown should be available, but treated with caution.

Benefits on death

The limits for occupational schemes, for what can be given on death, are the same as for final-salary schemes and are explained in Appendix 1.

The NAPF survey shows that 53 per cent of members are covered for four times salary, with another 26 per cent getting between three and four times. A few schemes vary the amount according to length of service, and nearly a quarter of members have a higher lump sum if they are married than if they are single (to pay for the cost of buying a spouse's pension).

How to tell if you are in a good scheme

A good scheme will provide a lump sum death benefit of four times earnings. Otherwise, there should be a separate life insur-ance policy, to top up the accumulated fund in order to bring the

spouse's pension up to a specific fraction of the member's pay –
say, 30 per cent.

If only the minimum spouse's pension is bought with the
Protected Rights fund (explained on page 39) then for a young
spouse of someone who has only been in the scheme for a few
years, that will be very small indeed.

It will be very much cheaper for the employer to take out a group
policy covering everyone – older and younger, healthy and less
healthy – than for each person to have to find his or her own benefit.
It will also ensure that everyone is covered, whereas only the
prudent will take action for themselves. So it should be a priority,
even if you cannot persuade the employer to make much of a
contribution to the pension itself.

Early leavers

The legal requirements for leavers from occupational schemes are
explained in Chapters 5 and 8, and few schemes would do anything
except the minimum.

Many providers make a PP 'paid up' once a certain number of
contributions have been missed, perhaps three months' worth.
With an ordinary personal pension, they will then deduct charges,
and leave the fund to grow. In some cases, the paid up value during
the first few years is very low, or even non-existent because of the
level of charges. In many cases, it is possible to reinstate the policy
later. Though there may be a charge, it is usually cheaper than the
alternative of starting a new policy.

With a *stakeholder* pension, however, whether you are still paying
contributions or not, by law the deductions cannot be more than 1
per cent of the fund each year (and may be less in some cases). You
cannot be penalized for stopping and starting contributions as you
wish. Some personal pensions now follow the same pattern.

Transfers from a personal/stakeholder scheme

It is possible to transfer to another personal or stakeholder scheme,
or into an occupational pension. An ordinary personal pension
scheme, though, may penalize you even more heavily for transferring out than for remaining paid up. A stakeholder scheme is not
allowed to do so – you must be free to move your money elsewhere,
at no charge.

How to tell if you are in a good scheme

The main issue is the charges. Press for the scheme to be on 'stakeholder terms' so far as early leavers are concerned – that is, no penalties for stopping contributions or for transferring.

An older GPP may still be using the old scale of charges. Check this out, and press the employer to renegotiate (with the help of a benefit consultant, if necessary). Cut-throat competition in the pensions industry means that a threat to move altogether, or to start a new contract with someone else even if leaving the existing framework in place, can have a considerable effect.

Many older GPPs were set up on the basis of a 'special deal' on charges while someone worked for a particular employer, but with those charges reverting to the normal scales as soon as the person left. Often, the wording was deliberately obscure to disguise this. Ask detailed questions about this and don't give up without a clear answer. Again, the employer should be able to renegotiate if the terms are poor.

What standard to look for?

As explained at the beginning of this chapter, the key question with any money-purchase scheme is how much money is going into it. But what makes a money-purchase scheme good or bad?

Some examples are given by actuary Bryn Davies, in his TUC booklet (*Getting the Best from Defined Contribution Schemes*; see Appendix 2 for details). They apply both to occupational schemes or GPPs.

Poor scheme

▪ Contracted out of SERPS, but with only the minimum NI rebates required by law going in.

▪ Employer provides separate insurance to pay for spouses' benefits on death in service, but limited to one times salary at death.

▪ On early retirement, a pension is available at a reduced level. Pension increases are the minimum required by law.

Standard scheme

▊ Contracted out of SERPS, with the employer and employee paying matching contributions, perhaps 5–6 per cent each, rising with age.

▊ Separate arrangements for spouses' benefits, worth two times salary at time of death and can be used to buy a spouse's pension.

▊ Reduced pension on early retirement; member can decide whether to take a lower annuity on retirement to pay for pension increases at a later date.

High quality scheme

▊ Based on target pension of two-thirds of final pay, with the scheme actuary calculating how much the contributions need to be, and the employer meeting the cost of the contributions and all the administration costs.

▊ Separate insurance to pay for spouses' benefits, which will be worth five times salary at time of death, and out of which the spouse's pension will be bought.

▊ Separate PHI policy pays for ill health benefits, and guarantees a proportion of earnings will be paid up to retirement age.

▊ Pension is increased in line with inflation each year.

10 Building up extra pension

Whatever sort of pension arrangement you are in, you have the chance to build up extra pension, up to the IR's limits for your type of scheme (see Appendix 1).

Increasing an occupational pension scheme

In an occupational scheme, the possibilities are:

▌ paying Additional Voluntary Contributions (AVCs) to a contract set up by the scheme trustees – though it will probably be run by an outside body, such as an insurance company or a building society; or

▌ in the public sector, buying 'added years' from the scheme itself; or

▌ paying 'free-standing' AVCs (FSAVC) to an outside body which doesn't have a contract with your trustees;

▌ (with some exceptions) paying into a personal pension/stakeholder scheme.

You can choose more than one of these options at a time.

Additional Voluntary Contributions

Additional Voluntary Contributions (AVCs) can be paid by anyone who is a member of an occupational pension scheme. All schemes must have at least one arrangement available for you to pay into. The top limit on contributions is 15 per cent of your earnings for the main scheme and the AVCs added together. There is full tax relief.

Almost always, you buy a money-purchase pension with AVCs. You build up a 'pot' of money (as with a personal pension), and then it is used to buy an annuity – and give you some tax-free cash if you are entitled to any – when you start to draw it. In many larger schemes, you buy the annuity within the scheme itself. Sometimes this is at specially subsidized rates. More often, it is at a rate worked out by the actuary but still better than you can find on the market because the scheme is not making a profit from you.

In other cases, you can choose to buy the annuity either with the provider that has been running the scheme, or with another provider on the market. This is called the 'open market option' and was explained on page 113.

The pensions from both the main scheme and the AVCs, taken together, must not go over the IR's limits. As well as increasing your own pension, you can also use AVCs to buy increases in pension, up to the rise in the RPI or at a fixed rate, and a spouse's pension of two-thirds of one's own, along with a guarantee that the pension will be paid for at least 10 years. It may be possible to take your AVC pension earlier or later than the main scheme pension, though not all scheme rules allow this.

Anyone who puts in too much in additional contributions to benefit from them in full will be given a refund, less 33 per cent tax (49 cent if on the 40 per cent rate) when he or she retires. However, the IR does not want people to 'overfund' themselves deliberately, so the scheme administrator will do regular 'head-room checks', and not let you pay in so much that you are likely to end up with a pension above the limits.

For anyone who started paying AVCs after 7 April 1987, the money can only be used for a pension, and not for buying an extra tax-free lump sum at retirement. People who were already paying into AVC schemes before that date retain the right to a lump sum even if the employer is taken over, or changes the arrangement about who should provide them. But if the members themselves change jobs, they lose this right for further payments. These rules do not bite very often, however, because many people are able to take the full lump sum by commuting their pension from the main scheme (explained in Chapter 8) and using the AVC pension to replace what has been given up.

The trustees set up the AVC contract, and should keep an eye on it. This means that the charges for AVCs should be low, compared to other insurance products. In many cases, the company anyway carries these. With stakeholder pensions coming on the scene, the charges should have come down much further – by around half in many cases, according to one survey. There are schemes, though, that give poor value to members, especially for people putting in relatively small contributions with only a few years to go before retirement. In most cases, this is because the employer has been using a financial adviser who charges commission and this has bumped up the cost.

Good AVC arrangements also give members a choice of investments. These might include a with-profits policy with an insurance company, a choice of their 'managed funds', or a building society deposit account. There are, though, some that only offer one investment. This may be linked to the main pension fund or it may be a single contract with one insurance company. This is fine if the investment does well, but not so good if it does badly.

Action points

Find out what the charges are on your scheme's AVC arrangements, and who bears them – is it the scheme, or the AVC-holding members?

If it is the members, look at how the charges are set up. Do they bear more heavily on people who make small contributions than on those making large ones? Press the trustees to renegotiate the contract. They should be able to do this on a 'nil-commission' basis, if they use one of the big firms of specialist consultants that do a lot of this.

Check what happens when the member retires and an annuity has to be bought with the AVC pot: is the member getting the best value for money?

Check the investment choice and how well it is explained to the members. If necessary, you and your fellow members could press the trustees to bring in another provider.

Added years

In public sector schemes like those in the Civil Service or local government, you can buy extra years of entitlement in your main scheme, so long as you can meet various detailed conditions (which vary between the different schemes). The extra benefits you have bought are treated in the same way as the main pension, including being inflation-proofed both before and after retirement.

This makes them quite expensive and not suitable for everyone. If you are not married, for instance, there is not much point in spending money to buy extra spouse's pension. Anyone eligible, though, should enquire about how many years he or she could buy and the cost, even if he or she then plumps for an ordinary AVC.

Free-standing AVCs

You are entitled to pay into a free-standing AVC (FSAVC) scheme, run by some other provider, up to the same limits as for the main scheme. However, you can never have tax-free cash from an FSAVC. You will pay the cost of setting up the policy, and usually also pay commission to the seller. It's estimated that these costs can eat up 20 per cent of contributions during the lifetime of a policy.

The total of the main scheme pension, and that from AVCs and FSAVCs must still not go above the IR limits. An individual can put up to £2,400 a year into the FSAVC scheme without any need to cross-check with the employer. However, the pension scheme administrator should calculate how much 'headroom' there is for extra benefits, and to make this possible the FSAVC provider has to notify the main scheme that someone has taken a contract out with them.

The number of cases where it has ever been worthwhile to take out an FSAVC has been limited, and there were strong suspicions that there was some hard selling going on. The FSA has instructed providers to carry out a review, with a deadline for completion of 30 June 2002.

Action point

Anyone with an FSAVC policy ought to check whether it is worthwhile continuing. Even if you lose money by surrendering the policy or making it paid up, you may end up with a better bargain by doing so and starting to pay into the in-house AVC, or a personal/stakeholder scheme (if you are eligible) instead.

Paying into a personal or stakeholder pension

Members of occupational pension schemes earning less than £30,000 a year are allowed to take out a personal/stakeholder pension at the same time, paying in up to £3,600 a year. They can then have the pension from this *on top* of the maximum pension allowed by the IR. They will also be able to obtain a lump sum on retirement.

However, the IR has made different arrangements for obtaining the tax relief, depending on whether you have an AVC or a personal/stakeholder pension. With an AVC, as with the main scheme pension, the tax relief comes 'at source', because the pension contribution is paid out of your gross pay. With a personal/stakeholder pension, you pay out of your *net* (take-home) pay and the provider then reclaims the tax from the IR.

Many employers are saying that they cannot deal with making two sorts of pension deductions from people's pay at the same time. So if you want to take out a stakeholder pension on top of your occupational scheme, you have to do it all yourself. Other employers have found it possible, though, to run both systems.

Action points

Check whether your pension scheme's communication material explains that there is more than one option.

Ask your union, if there is one, to negotiate with the employer to offer a direct deduction facility to members of the occupational scheme, as well as those who are not members, for payments to the designated stakeholder scheme.

Special note. If yours is one of the few *occupational* pension schemes that is being treated for tax purposes as if it is a *personal* one, this chance to put in £3,600 above the ordinary tax limits is not open to you. You are stuck with the personal pension contribution limits, though you can mix-and-match as many different varieties of pension, within those limits, as you like.

Other ways of buying extra pension

It is possible to 'sacrifice' some of your salary or bonus to buy extra pension, as explained on page 169. Doing this too late in a career can be dangerous, however, because it would reduce the final earnings on which the pension would be calculated. A redundancy or severance payment may also be sacrificed. It's important to get specialist advice on any sort of sacrifice.

Increasing a personal/stakeholder pension

There are no AVCs as such with this sort of pension. Instead, you simply make contributions each year to the IR's limits, explained in Appendix 1.

A good GPP, or any stakeholder scheme, will be flexible enough to allow you to do this, and also to put in lump sums when it suits you – perhaps from a bonus or arrears of pay after a settlement.

Some older GPPs, and many personal pensions that people have bought for themselves penalize you not just if you reduce your contributions, but if you *increase* them as well! Their argument is that it involves extra administration, but really it is just a way of taking more money from you in a way you may not notice. If you are stuck with a policy like this:

▪ get advice on whether it would be better to cut your losses and stop paying in altogether, or just carry on paying what you are committed to;

▪ if the latter, start up a stakeholder policy as well, and pay any extra contributions into that instead;

▪ ask the union, if there is one, to press the employer to use its bargaining power to renegotiate the GPP contract.

11 *Getting information about your pension*

Occupational pensions

Since occupational schemes are set up under trust law (explained on page 47), the beneficiaries of those trusts – that is, the members and those who might be paid benefits – are entitled to know what is going on. Various pieces of tax and social security legislation have brought in more rights. Many of these were brought together in one place in the Occupational Pension Schemes (Disclosure of Information) Regulations 1996 (Statutory Instrument 1996 No 1655). Other parts of the Pensions Act also required other types of information to be given. Since 1996, there have been further changes, with more elements of information available.

For more details, look at *Disclosure Made Simple*, published by NAPF (see Appendix 2 for details). It isn't simple, but they have had a good try at making it so.

Basic information about the scheme

This must be given automatically to prospective members (those who have a right to join but haven't yet done so) and to new members who have not already received it, within two months of joining. Any member or prospective member's spouse or beneficiary and recognized trade unions are also entitled to ask for any of this information, and it must be given within two months. If there is a 'material change' in the information (say, a benefit improvement) then the trustees must notify members before it takes place, or within three months afterwards.

The main information to be provided is:

∎   who is eligible to join;

∎ what the conditions of membership are, the amount of notice you have to give if you want to opt out, and whether you can come back into the scheme – if so, on what conditions;

∎ how members' and employers' contributions are calculated;

∎ whether the scheme is contracted out of SERPS/S2P;

∎ what the benefits are and how they are calculated, and whether any of them are at the discretion of the trustees;

∎ details of where to go with further enquiries, and an explanation of the internal disputes procedure (see Chapter 15).

Usually, all this is put in a single pension scheme booklet, but there is no rule to say it must all be in one place.

The scheme's basic working documents are the trust deed and rules. These have to be made available for inspection at a 'reasonable' place. Members, recognized trade unions and others can also ask to be given copies. They can be charged for this, but only for the cost of copying, packing and posting the documents.

The trust deed and rules usually override the scheme booklet, if there is a difference between them. But if there has been an announcement of a change, which has not yet been included in the rules but is intended to, this could have the same effect. Just what the position is in a particular case has been the source of some lucrative – for the lawyers – court cases in recent years.

There is also a right to know the names and addresses of all the employers in the scheme.

Information to individual members

In a salary-related scheme, current and deferred members have a right to know what their benefits would be at retirement or on death if they ask, but not automatically. If they have already been told within the last 12 months, they need not be told again.

In a money-purchase scheme, the member must automatically be told what contributions have been credited in the course of the year, how the fund has built up and how much of it is Protected Rights (explained on page 39), and what the transfer value would be. At present, this need only be in money terms, which is not very useful for trying to work out whether you will have enough to live on in 40 years' time. So from April 2003, the Government plans to make schemes produce 'real terms' illustrations of the future benefits – that is, showing what you would get in terms of today's money (which may come as a nasty shock to many people in money-purchase schemes).

All this information is usually in the Annual Benefit Statement, which most schemes send out automatically to members each year. The Government has a project for 'combined benefit forecasts', which will include details of your state pension as well as your occupational (or personal/stakeholder) pension. It is hoping that most large schemes will sign up for these within the next few years.

People should be given details of what pension they will get, and how it is worked out, either before or shortly after they start to draw it. The scheme must also explain about the conditions of payment, and any provisions under which the pension could be altered. So, for instance, a widow receiving a pension for the first time must be told if she could lose it by remarrying. New details must be given if the amount of pension changes, unless it is simply being uprated in line with an annual formula.

If someone dies, the surviving spouse or other beneficiaries must be told the details of their rights and options, and the way that any pension will be increased, within two months.

Anyone leaving the scheme must be given details of their rights and options. (See Chapter 5 for details of the information that must be given about transfers, and the time limits.)

If the scheme is being wound up, details of the amount of benefit due, and who will be responsible for paying it, must go to every beneficiary and every member who has an entitlement. If there's a shortfall in the benefit, they must be informed.

The annual report

Trustees (but not public sector schemes without trustees) have to draw up an annual report, including audited accounts. The report must be given to any members, spouses, beneficiaries, prospective members and recognized trade unions that ask for it. Many schemes also produce a short 'popular' version or include edited highlights in a newsletter, which goes out to everyone, leaving those who want the full version to request it.

The report has to include:

▌ a report from the trustees;

▌ the audited accounts;

▌ a statement from the actuary;

▌ an investment report.

The report from the trustees has to give some basic information about the way the scheme is run, including details of the trustees and the advisers, and statistics about scheme members and pensioners. It is a good place to look for help in understanding how the scheme is set up and who does what.

In the scheme accounts, there are two main tables. These are the revenue account, that is, an explanation of what money has come in and gone out over the last year; and an analysis of the *assets* held by the scheme. This is not quite the same as the balance sheet that you would see in the company's accounts, because the liabilities – the amount that the scheme expects to pay out in due course as pensions – are missing. These are dealt with in the actuary's statement. There must also be an explanation of changes in the assets, where these don't show up in the revenue account. For example, this section has to show how the market value of the shares has gone up or down.

The other important item in the annual report, for a salary-related scheme, is the actuarial statement. It is, though, fairly limited in what it shows, and you really need a copy of the full valuation to see how well funded or otherwise the scheme is. The statement has to say, first, whether the actuary thinks there is enough money in the scheme to cover the liabilities that have built up so far. This is on the assumption that the scheme closes down and all the members are treated as early leavers. Second, the actuary has to say whether he or she thinks that 'the resources of the scheme are likely in the normal course of events to meet in full the liabilities of the scheme as they fall due'. There is then a summary of the contribution rates expected from the employer and employees, and details of the assumptions being made.

The annual report and accounts must be produced seven months after the end of the pension scheme year. So for a scheme with a year-end of 6 April, the report should be ready by 7 November. It's an offence under the Pensions Act to be late with the report, and the trustees may be fined. Opra takes it particularly seriously because, it says, late reporting can be an indicator that other things are wrong with the scheme, or at least that there is sloppy management.

Other documents

There is a right to see various other documents that the scheme has to produce under the Pensions Act. These are:

▌ the actuarial valuation report;

▌ the schedule of contributions or schedule of payments;

▌ the statement of investment principles.

As with the trust deed, you can either inspect these at a 'reasonable place', or be sent copies, for which you can be charged.

There are some things you do not have a right to know. If some people in the scheme have different levels of benefits (for instance, senior executives), you do not have a right to find out about these. You don't have the right to see the minutes of trustee meetings. However, under much older trust law, you can argue that you should at least be able to see minutes about decisions affecting you. Some decisions by the Pensions Ombudsman seem to be going in the same direction. You'll never get the right to see confidential material about other people, or them about you.

The accounts have to give figures for the different categories of investment, and whether it's in the UK or overseas, but not which company's shares the pension fund owns or in what countries. A few schemes publish full details; for example, the Universities' Superannuation Scheme (USS) lists them in full on its Web site.

Action points

You and your fellow scheme members might consider asking the union, if you have one, to check whether the pension scheme booklet is clear and understandable, and kept up to date. It's worthwhile testing out the material on new recruits to the scheme to see how well they grasp it.

If your scheme does not provide an automatic benefit statement, press for it to do so. If everyone made one-off requests for information, it would be much more trouble for the scheme to deal with them than sending out material automatically.

In a money-purchase scheme, check whether it gives you predictions of what your benefit will be in real terms, including a forecast of what proportion of your pay it might be. If not, check when they are going to start doing this. Find out whether your scheme is going to cooperate in the Government's 'combined benefit forecasts' project, and if not, why not.

Press for the scheme to send out a 'popular' report, or announce changes in a user-friendly style. Ask the scheme to submit its documents to the Plain English Campaign, which awards the 'Crystal Mark' for clarity, or to one of the rival organizations doing the same job. They charge a fee, but it is worthwhile for the improvement you will see in the documents.

There's a trend now to put pensions material on the company's internal Internet (the intranet). Some of the Web sites are much better than others. The trustees should ask ordinary members, especially people who are not computer-literate, to say what they think about yours. It's worthwhile getting some additional value into the sites, such as a 'what-if' calculator so that people can see what would happen to benefits if they increased their contributions, and links through to other useful sites.

Going electronic creates problems for those who don't have ready access to a computer in work time. People would be able to challenge the scheme about this, if it meant that some groups of members were unable to exercise their rights to information. Paper-based material ought still to be made available.

The unions should build up a library of all the pensions material – the detailed trust deeds, annual reports and valuations, and all the announcements and booklets sent out as well. Keep back-files of documents produced in previous years. This will help if the people negotiating pensions are ever in dispute with the employer or trustees about what was said, for instance about the likely level of a benefit in the future.

Try to get the employer to agree a time limit on queries being answered, better than the legal requirement. Two months is far too long.

The point to make is that if members do not understand the scheme, they will not value it. Indeed, they may be suspicious if they feel that the employer is somehow trying to pull the wool over their eyes. Running a scheme is not cheap for the employer, and so it is 'spoiling the ship for a ha'porth of tar' to be mean about spending money on communication.

Personal and stakeholder pensions

You have rights to information about a personal pension, and some extra rights if it is classified as a stakeholder scheme. Giving the information is the job of the scheme provider – the insurance company or other body – rather than the employer. The providers may use the employer, or an independent financial adviser, to distribute the information, however. There are no requirements for the unions to be given information.

Basic information on the scheme

This has to be supplied within 13 weeks to the member, if he or she has not already been given it within the last three years. The spouse or other beneficiary can also ask for information, but need only be given what is relevant to them. Any alterations should be notified, where possible, three months before they happen.

The information covered under this requirement is:

▮ conditions of membership;

▮ how and where to obtain the full constitution of the scheme (you have a right to inspect these documents at a 'reasonable' place, or to buy copies);

▮ how contributions by members, the employer and National Insurance Contributions Office (if you are contracted out) are paid;

▮ the conditions for transferring the money, buying an annuity, or taking a lump sum;

▮ a summary of the investment policy;

▮ estimates of what would be available to transfer if you chose to move within five years;

▮ the charges, and what will be paid in commission;

▮ the benefits covered by insurance policies, and what would happen if the insurer did not have the resources to pay the Protected Rights benefit;

▮ details of where to get further information, and how to make a complaint.

Anyone with a personal pension should be sent an annual statement of what is in the fund. If your employer is making direct deductions from your pay, these statements have to show how much was passed to the insurer and the date. In due course, there should also be illustrations in 'real' terms (after taking account of inflation) as explained above.

Anyone coming up to retirement should be sent a statement of what they will be entitled to. If there is an 'open market option' (explained on page 113) for buying your annuity, this must be spelt out.

Stakeholder pensions

There are some additional rights if a personal pension is registered as a stakeholder scheme. It has to send every member, once a year, a statement showing how much was there at the beginning of the scheme year, and how it has changed over the year because of investment gains or losses, contributions coming in, and any other payments out. There must also be a statement of what the charges are, as a percentage of the fund. For the few schemes that are set up under trustees (such as the one the TUC is running) there are also rights to see the trust deed, statement of investment principles and so on, as for an occupational scheme.

Action points

Usually, all the general information is given in a brochure or 'policy document'. It often looks very attractive, but turns out to be full of small print and gobbledegook once you start reading it. There is a joint project among insurance companies called 'Raising Standards' which is aimed at improving the way they communicate and administer their products. Check whether the particular insurance company is subscribing to this. Look also for the Plain English Campaign's 'Crystal Mark' or something similar.

There will usually be a Web site. Some are very good, but some are dreadful. See whether there are calculation tools you can make use of, and other links.

If yours is a GPP or a stakeholder scheme set up for a group, you will have some influence because the group could 'vote with their feet' by moving elsewhere – and at least for a stakeholder scheme, meet no penalties. Tell the contact person your company has within the provider – perhaps called the Client Manager or Customer Relations Manager – what you think is wrong. If the employer and the union, if there is one, are just at the start of looking for a scheme (see Chapter 9), press them to take the way they communicate into account. It will say something about their overall attitude.

12 Changes to your pension arrangements

Occupational schemes

Section 67

Section 67 of the Pensions Act is a major safeguard for scheme members against their employer changing their pension scheme. It restricts any changes that could affect any entitlements or 'accrued rights' of the members. This means the benefits to which the members would be entitled if they left the scheme just before the change. So it includes pension increases that are guaranteed in the rules, but not those given at the trustees' discretion, and it does not include the lump sum death benefit, since that disappears if you leave the scheme. However, one recent legal case in Scotland, *Larsen's Executrix*, means that employers cannot simply assume that they can withdraw death benefits without warning.

If any amendment might affect entitlements or accrued rights, the trustees have to satisfy themselves, before making it, that either an actuary has given a certificate that the amendment is not detrimental, or the members' consent has been obtained.

This would mean sending out letters to those affected. If someone does not respond to a letter about a change, in some circumstances that can be regarded as consent. However, trustees are not able to impose a detrimental amendment on an individual member from whom they have not heard.

If a retrospective change can only benefit people – for instance, improving the accrual rate from 1/80th to 1/70th for past as well as future service – then Section 67 will not come into play. More often, however, a change will be detrimental to some people, even if it is beneficial to most. So the trustees would generally need to ask the actuary to identify who might be affected, and to go through the Section 67 procedure for those people.

Section 67 does not apply to changes to future benefits.

Contracted out occupational schemes

There are consultation rights for a contracted out occupational scheme, which are given in the Social Security Pensions Act 1975. If a contracted out scheme is amended to contracted in, or a contracted in scheme is amended to contracted out, or a contracted out scheme is amended in a way that affects, or might affect, the terms of contracting out, then the employer must give three months' notice to the members. This period can be shortened to a month if the unions agree in writing. The employer must also 'consult' the recognized trade unions. The National Insurance Contributions Office (NICO), which is part of the IR, then has to give its consent. Individuals and the unions have a right to complain to NICO if they believe the requirements have not been met – but so far as anyone knows, they have never refused a certificate on those grounds.

If the scheme is being amended so that it is no longer contracted out, there are rules to ensure that the GMPs or Protected Rights funds already built up are safeguarded.

What the IR allows

The IR will allow occupational schemes to be altered, but for anything major it has to give its approval. For some lesser items, it allows the scheme's lawyers to use standard clauses and send in a 'documentation certificate'. Making an alteration without its blessing may jeopardize the scheme's tax status.

Your rights under scheme trust deeds

The way the rules of a particular scheme are changed will depend on what the original trust deed says. Many trust deeds provide very broad powers for the trustees or the employer (or the one with the other's consent) to amend the rules. If the amendment is likely to cost money, the trustees may have to ask the scheme actuary either to confirm that the scheme is affordable or to say what extra contribution is needed.

Some trust deeds give extra protection to the members. They might have to be given notice before an amendment is made, or they might have the right to vote on it, though this is rare. Other deeds safeguard future benefits as well as past ones. Lloyds Bank came unstuck on this issue a few years ago, when it tried to remove the rights of a group of its staff to early retirement, and found that the trust deed would not let it do so. There have been other cases where it turned out that amendments had not been properly made, so that they were invalid, or where the effect was different from what the employer intended. It is always worth checking just what the trust deed says. If need be, ask the union to get legal advice, just in case the company has been pushing its luck!

In terms of the contract of employment, most scheme booklets will include a clause saying something like, 'Although it is intended that the scheme will continue in its present form, we reserve the right to amend or terminate it at any time.' This would generally safeguard the employer against contractual claims. You *might* be able to argue that a change is a 'fundamental' change in your contract of employment (as with retirement ages, explained in Chapter 3), or that the employer has broken the relationship of trust and confidence you are entitled to have. If you left as a result, you could then claim constructive dismissal. You might also be able to claim that the employer had broken promises to you. However, it would be very difficult to make a case of this sort – apart from anything else, because people do not leave their jobs just because of their pension scheme. So in practice legal protection for future benefits is rather weak.

On top of this, it's always open to the employer to wind up the scheme altogether and start again with a different sort of pension scheme or just offering stakeholder access. Generally, keeping the scheme, even with a reduced level of benefits, would be better than that.

Personal/stakeholder schemes

Since GPPs and stakeholder pensions involve a contract between the provider (usually an insurance company) and the individual, the procedure for changes depends on contract law and what the policy documents say. Sometimes the meaning of these documents is very contentious, and there has to be a court case to sort things out – as people with Equitable Life policies know to their cost.

It is the individual's decision whether to contract out or not. He or she can change his or her mind at any time, by filling in a form that the provider should supply.

What a good arrangement would include

You and your fellow scheme members could consider asking the union to press for any changes to be negotiated with the unions or staff representatives; see Chapter 6 for more details. If the scheme is changing its contracted out status, they can make use of the formal notice and consultation requirements to push for discussion.

Sometimes the proposal is for a set of alterations that are generally beneficial, but will make a few people worse off. The aim should be, though, that no one individual should be worse off. The union should not ask people to sign away their Section 67 rights. With the lump sum death benefit, where the protection is weaker, at least the *money* amount should stay the same. For example, it might be agreed to reduce the lump sum from four times to three times earnings, in return for an increased spouse/dependant's pension. If Joe Smith's earnings are £20,000, so that he is currently insured for £80,000, he should remain insured for that figure, until his earnings have increased enough to mean that he will get more than that under the three-times earnings figure.

Closing one scheme and starting another

This is often the easiest way to make a major change. For example, in the Civil Service the old pension scheme is being closed in October 2002, with a new one starting up on the same day. They are both final-salary schemes, though, so it is easy for members to see what is happening.

In other cases, there may be a change in the type of scheme being offered. A number of large employers are closing their final-salary schemes to new recruits, and starting up a money-purchase scheme for them. Sainsbury's, Marks & Spencer and Lattice (formerly part of British Gas) have all recently said they are doing this. Occasionally, this involves opening up a new section in the original scheme, especially if the employer wants to make use of surplus cash to pay its share of the contributions for new entrants – essentially, subsidizing the new scheme. The judges in the *Barclays Bank v Holmes* case in 2000, decided that this was legal so long as the trust deed allowed it. Lawyers warned that 'employers should be wary of setting up a new section without checking their drafting thoroughly'. The unions would certainly want to trip them up if they could!

The first point is to be clear what 'closing' the scheme means. It can mean:

▮ closing it to new recruits, but letting existing staff stay in the scheme, for as long as they want – though they are usually offered the chance to transfer;

▮ closing it both for new recruits and for building up future accruals. The pension stays where it is. If it is a salary-related scheme, when someone retires their pension is calculated on their salary at retirement, but no more years of service build up. Again, people are usually offered the chance to transfer;

▮ closing it down altogether, so that people have the choice of transferring, having a 'bought out' deferred pension, or buying their own personal/stakeholder pension. This may not happen immediately the new scheme comes into existence, but could arise a few years down the line, when the old scheme is dwindling in numbers and becoming expensive and awkward to administer.

There is some legal protection if the company wants people to transfer to the new scheme. It is only possible to transfer people without their consent, if:

▮ both schemes are run by the same employer or connected employers, or if a group of people are being transferred because of a take-over or sell-off; and

▮ the receiving scheme's actuaries certify to the trustees of the transferring scheme that the rights being bought by the members with the transfer credits are 'no less favourable, broadly speaking, than those in the transferring scheme'; and

▮ there is 'good cause' for believing that established customs for discretionary benefits would be broadly the same. This means, particularly, what sort of pension increases will be given.

Actuaries are very wary of certifying this, so very few of these transfers happen. It is far more usual to 'make an offer you can't refuse'. This might say that if you transfer within, perhaps, three months, you will get full back-service rights, and possibly even some credits, whereas if you leave your deferred pension in the old scheme, or decide to transfer later, you get only what an ordinary early leaver would have had.

What a good employer would do

The best position is that the previous scheme carries on running for as long as there are people who want to belong to it, and that there is a free choice – kept open indefinitely – for members to move across for future service.

They should be able to take a separate decision on whether to take their past service rights across also, or leave them with the old scheme. If they transfer, they should be given year-for-year credits in the new scheme, or even better than year-for-year if the new package is worse.

Very often, the right choice for members will vary according to their age and their job prospects. For example, a young high-flyer is more likely to benefit from moving between schemes, for both past and future service, than an older person in a job without much prospect of pay increases. So individuals should be given full information about their comparable benefits in the two schemes, and the chance to have a one-to-one discussion with someone in a position to know what they are talking about – from a firm of benefit consultants, for instance – about what is bothering them.

The union ought to be fully consulted about all the information to be provided, with the chance to bring in their own experts if they wish (with the employer paying, if possible), but there should not be pressure to move, or a 'selling exercise'.

This is even more important if the two schemes are different in kind – if one is a final-salary occupational scheme and the other a money-purchase stakeholder scheme, for instance. Comparing the two types is like comparing apples and pears. A lot of time and effort needs to be spent on explaining to members, and helping them understand the choices.

An example: the Civil Service scheme

After several years of discussion and negotiation with the civil service unions, the new PCSPS 2000 scheme goes live in October 2002.

A new stakeholder scheme is being launched in parallel. New recruits will have a free choice about joining this or the new DB scheme. Existing members have the choice of remaining in the current PCSPS scheme, moving across to the new DB scheme for future service only, or moving past service entitlement also, with each year in the old scheme counting as slightly less than a year in the new. This choice, though, will only last on these terms for a few months – after that, transfers will still be possible, but on less favourable terms.

Every civil servant was sent a letter from the Head of the Civil Service, and four fact sheets with general information. As the transfer date came closer, a personalized statement of their individual options, a question and answer booklet, and a personalized workbook have been sent out. All the material has been checked with the Plain English Campaign and has its Crystal Mark. People who return their 'Choice' forms are even being entered into a prize draw.

If the old scheme is being closed for future service, or closed altogether, this means that, so far as the future is concerned, people will only have the alternatives of joining the new scheme or making their own provision outside the company. As explained on page 30, the employer can even refuse to give them access to the designated stakeholder scheme, if there is an occupational scheme that they could have joined in the past but did not do so.

Almost always, it is better to join the new scheme for future service than not to do so. The only exception might be if it were a very poor money-purchase scheme where you are forced to contract out (a COMP scheme, explained on page 38). Even if the pension is not worth much, having the lump sum death benefit will usually be worthwhile.

Transferring the pension built up for past service, however, is a different matter. The key question will be how generous the transfer terms are. If you are going between salary-related schemes, a good package would be:

■ year-for-year (or better) credits in the new scheme – so that if you had 10 years' service in the old one, you have at least 10 years' service in the new one too;

■ protection for any other benefits in the old scheme that are better than those in the new one;

■ a 'no worse off' calculation – ideally, indefinitely, but at least for the next few years so that those coming up to retirement are protected. That is, the pension for the service transferred from the previous scheme is calculated on the basis used for that old scheme, and also on the basis used for the new one, and the better benefit paid.

The keener the employer is for people to transfer, the more it should be willing to pay to provide safeguards, so ensure they do.

If the new scheme is money-purchase – whether it is occupational, a GPP, or a stakeholder scheme – people need to be very cautious indeed about taking a transfer rather than leaving a deferred pension in the old scheme. The FSA says that if the transfer is into any sort of personal or stakeholder scheme, the adviser needs to do a 'transfer value analysis' for the members, to show whether it is worthwhile. This isn't a requirement for an occupational scheme, but press for it to be done anyway. If the company is keen to transfer people into the new arrangement, they will probably have to provide substantial extra money (or possibly take it out of the surplus, see page 144) to ensure that even with bad investment returns, people don't lose out.

Whatever the type of new scheme, a good employer should provide individual statements showing what each person will get as a deferred pension or as a transfer. Also request a 'surgery', with qualified financial advisers paid for by the company, at which anyone can have a one-to-one consultation about what is best for him or her. If this is not possible, or not for remote sites, a telephone helpline is better than nothing – though many people find it difficult to take in detailed information given on the phone. If the company has an in-house Internet (intranet), they ought to create a section that allows people to do 'what-if' calculations about their own futures.

If the unions or member representatives have negotiated the terms, and are satisfied with what they have achieved, a joint recommendation from both unions and employers will carry considerable weight. It would be sensible, though, for the union to ask for advice from a specialist, probably an actuary – and for representatives talking about the options not to go beyond the advice they are given. Otherwise, the union could find there was a claim for compensation against it!

It is important that everyone is asked to make a positive decision, one way or the other – that they must all sign something, and that the employer chases up those who don't sign. It will avoid disputes in the future if there is clear evidence of what the member's intentions were.

If the old scheme is being wound up altogether

What happens when a scheme is being wound up is covered in full in the next chapter. Here, we are only looking at the choices members will have if the company has a new scheme into which it wants the members to move.

The aims would be the same as in the last section, but the difference is that the members will not be able to keep a deferred pension in the old scheme. So their choices will be:

▮ transferring past service into the new scheme;

▮ taking a transfer value (explained in Chapter 5) from the old scheme and buying a personal/stakeholder pension; or

▮ having a deferred annuity bought for them by the trustees of the old scheme, when they wind it up completely.

The last two choices are both on a money-purchase basis. Anyone would need to be very careful before deciding that they are the better option than transferring into the new scheme on a basis of credited service – even if it was less than full service. This will make proper communication, and easily available advice, even more important.

13 **Winding up a scheme completely**

What you must have

Every set of trust deeds will have a long and complicated winding-up rule. The trustees will be responsible for putting it into effect. Usually, wind up has to start automatically if the employer is going out of business. There will also be provisions to allow the employer to force a winding up, either by giving notice to the trustees that they must do so, or by refusing to pay the right contributions so that the trustees have to start the process.

If the scheme is contracted out of SERPS/S2P, the employer must *inform* the members, by giving them a 'notice of intention', and *consult* the recognized trade unions. When the time comes to wind up the scheme, the trustees must buy the right sort of insurance policies for the members, so that their GMPs or Protected Rights (explained in Chapter 4) are covered.

The trustees have to distribute the assets according to the rules. They can do this by transferring them to another scheme, or they can buy them out by taking out insurance policies – immediate annuities for the pensioners, deferred annuities for everyone else. What *can't* happen, though, is for the members to get a cash payout in their hands. The money set aside for their pensions must always go into some other pension arrangement.

In a money-purchase scheme, the amount to be distributed and how it is divided between the members, is clear because it is simply the value of each person's pension 'pot'. For a final-salary or hybrid scheme, though, even if the scheme is well funded on an ongoing basis, there can be a shortfall when it comes to be wound up. Section 73 of the Pensions Act, and the regulations linked with it, then come into play. These *override* any different rules in the trust deed and lay down a priority order for payouts:

■ costs and expenses;

■ benefits from AVCs (covered in Chapter 10);

■ pensions already in payment, and potential spouses' pensions for those pensioners, but not future pension increases;

■ contracted out pension rights of all the various types;

■ pension increases for existing pensioners and contracted out rights;

■ other deferred pensions, and accrued pensions for current members.

This means that if there is a shortfall, the current and deferred members will bear the brunt of it – they could get nothing if all the money is used up on the pensioners. This would be particularly unfair on people who were only a few weeks or months from the safety of retirement. One saving grace is that if there is not enough money to pay GMPs built up before April 1997, the state will step in and pay these, and try to recover the money from the employer.

A shortfall in funding becomes a debt on the employer, but the employer is only required to make the fund up to 100 per cent of the Minimum Funding Requirement (MFR; see Glossary). This is not enough to give everyone full benefits on a wind up, so there will still be a gap. The Government is planning to strengthen the requirement in the near future, however. Even so, the debt is only an ordinary unsecured one, not a priority debt. In any company that is in trouble, the banks will probably have secured all the loans against the buildings and property, so there will be very little left over for the pension scheme to claim.

An example: Blagden

In 2000 a company called Blagden plc decided to go into voluntary liquidation. There was going to be a shortfall on the pension scheme when it wound up, and the trustees asked the company to pay £10.1 million. It could afford to do so, but decided to ask the shareholders what they thought, because this would mean less money for them. Several big shareholders – including other pension funds – voted down the arrangement. After some heavy pressure and publicity, especially from the chairman of the trustees, the company agreed to pay over £5.5 million, which was enough to secure the benefits.

> In some ways this was unusual, because very few solvent companies go into this sort of liquidation – most would not have the money in any case.

The final fallback, if there is a shortfall on the funds caused by 'fraud or misappropriation' is the Pensions Compensation Board. This can pay individuals' benefits while the scheme is sorted out, and then pay over a lump sum to wind up the scheme. No one needs to have been convicted of fraud for the PCB to come in, but the rules are quite tightly drawn, and so far it has taken on very few cases.

Winding up a scheme can take a very long time – four or five years is common, a decade or more is not unknown. The Government has brought in new regulations, taking effect in April 2002, to try to speed things up. The new law is being phased in to apply first to those schemes that have been winding up the longest. There will have to be regular reports to Opra about what is happening, and more contact with scheme members. This should at least mean that members are better informed.

Opra is publishing a guide to scheme wind ups that will be available from them or via their Web site (see Appendix 4).

Action points

If the company announces that it is closing the scheme down while still in business, the union representatives or a body of interested members ought to try to meet the employer and the trustees and establish:

- the reasons;
- whether there is any alternative, and if this has been properly thought through;
- what legal advice they have had;
- whether there is a surplus, and if they are trying to get hold of that; or
- if there is a shortfall, how bad this is and how much the company has to make it up.

A good employer will share the advice and calculations they have been given by their advisers. If there is a financial problem, there could be other ways round the issue. Could the scheme's future benefits be cut down, for example, rather than cut out altogether?

If there's a surplus

In some cases, there will be *more* money in the scheme than is needed to pay for all the benefits due – a 'surplus'. What happens then depends on what the scheme's trust deed says: the trustees may have discretion to increase the members' benefits, up to the limits allowed by the IR. Any surplus left above this goes to the company, after following a cumbersome procedure laid down under the Pensions Act 1995, and explained below.

Many trust deeds say that trustees need the employer's consent to increase the benefits. This means they have to negotiate with the employer about what share goes to whom. A few trust deeds say that the trustees must use any surplus to increase members' benefits, up to the IR's limit, before any surplus goes back to the employer.

Action points

If there is the possibility of a surplus payment, you and your fellow scheme members may want to press the union to check precisely your scheme's trust deed (see Chapter 11 for your rights to obtain information). Often the relevant clauses use the word 'determine' instead of 'terminate' or 'wind up'. This is just a bit of lawyers' jargon, but it can make it difficult to find the right section.

Try to negotiate to strengthen the members' position by saying that the members should have the maximum benefits first. It will not be easy to persuade the employer to weaken their own rights but it is worth trying. As far as the scheme members are concerned, it is their own money, and they have more of a moral right to it than the creditors or shareholders. However, if the company is already in trouble, the banks or other creditors may block a change of this sort.

For the company to obtain a surplus as part of a scheme wind up, the trustees must:

■ establish that they have met all the scheme's liabilities, including providing pension increases up to LPI level (explained on page 43);

■ use their discretion to make further increases, or decide not to do so; then

▌ inform all the scheme members that they plan to pay it over, giving them at least two months to write to Opra with any objections;

▌ check with Opra whether objections have been received, and then if they plan to go ahead, send out a second notice to the members saying that they will be extracting a payment within the next three months.

In some cases they may also need Opra to modify the scheme rules to allow them to have a surplus payment at all. Opra publishes a detailed technical guide to its requirements (see the address list in Appendix 4).

Action points

Consider pressing the union, if there is one, to start negotiating as early as possible. The employer may not want to discuss anything with the members, so you may find you can only communicate indirectly, via the trustees.

Though ideally most members would like the entire surplus to come to them and nothing to go to the company, in practice this is not realistic. A 50/50 split would be good, and members in many schemes have had to be satisfied with one-third, while the company gets the lion's share. The aim is for all the members, deferreds and pensioners to build up benefits as close to the IR limits as possible. If you cannot obtain enough, choices will need to be made about whether you want increases evenly spread or concentrated on the most deserving cases – perhaps the oldest pensioners.

If all the legal requirements have been met, Opra does not have the power to refuse a payment out. However, in some schemes there will be legal doubts about whether amendments have been properly carried out, or whether the trustees have always acted in line with the rules. If there are such questions, then Opra must refuse permission until these doubts have been resolved – which might mean going to the Ombudsman or the courts for a ruling.

Publicity can also be a useful weapon.

An example: McDermotts

Multinational oil-equipment company McDermotts is planning to pull out of the UK altogether. The unions representing ex-employees at the former Scottish construction site raised a series of issues about what the retirement age was in the scheme, what pensions should be paid on early retirement, and whether people had been correctly given or refused incapacity pensions. This meant that the payment to the employer was blocked. At the same time, the unions were campaigning via the Scottish newspapers and the Assembly to try to embarrass the company into treating its ex-employees better.

If the company is insolvent

When a company is insolvent, an 'insolvency practitioner' will be appointed to sort out its affairs. With a final-salary scheme, if the trustee board does not already include someone who is independent of the company, this person is responsible for appointing a special Independent Trustee (IT), unconnected with the employer or the practitioner. This will usually be a professional from one of the firms specializing in this.

This IT then takes over the powers of the trustee board. The IT will work out what benefits are due to each member on the wind up, and then buy 'deferred annuities' from insurance companies to cover these. If there is a surplus, the key question is what is laid down in the trust deed:

■   If the trustees have sole discretion to increase the members' benefits, up to the limits allowed by the IR, the IT will exercise this discretion.

■   If the trustees need the employer's consent to increase the benefits, the IT will negotiate with the insolvency practitioner about the division of the spoils. The more that goes to the pension scheme members, the less there will be for the company's creditors.

■   If you are lucky enough to have a trust deed saying that the trustees *must* use a surplus to increase members' benefits before anything goes to the employer, the insolvency practitioner will have to accept this. Only what's left after the members have been given maximum benefits will go to the creditors.

Any employees' contributions deducted but not paid over for the last 12 months can be claimed back from the National Insurance Fund if the money cannot be collected from the employer. Unpaid employer contributions can also be paid, but only the lowest of:

■ the unpaid contributions due for the last 12 months;

■ 10 per cent of employees' total pay during the last 12 months; and

■ (for a salary-related scheme) the amount certified by the actuary to be necessary to meet the scheme's liability to pay benefits.

Action points

You and your fellow scheme members should press the unions to move quickly. If you think a crash is coming, it will be important to have all the available information about the scheme, including a copy of the rules. Check what they say about winding up.

If the crash happens, arrange a meeting with the IT (or whoever is dealing with the wind up) and ask whether there is enough to pay all benefits, or if there will be a shortfall. If he or she doesn't yet have the information, ask how long it will be before this is done, and ask to be kept informed.

Everyone may then have to wait some time for things to be sorted out. The company's documents may be in chaos, and the lists of members' names and addresses may not be correct. So the union should make its own list, including dates of birth and marital status where possible, and give it to the person dealing with the wind up. Keep a copy, and give another to the union's full-time official or legal officer.

It is important that representatives keep in touch with whoever is doing the work. However, they will make a charge every time they answer a letter or talk to you on the phone, and this will come out of the scheme's funds, so no one should bother them unnecessarily. If there is a surplus in the scheme, try to negotiate for improving the benefits. There may be room for blocking action, as explained above on page 146.

Ultimately, the ex-members should be sent individual notification of their benefits, and the name of the insurance company with which they have been bought. It will be important to check that this has gone to everyone, and raise queries as soon as you can. Only when all these have been resolved will the scheme be completely wound up.

> In many cases, although the company is insolvent it is given permission to continue trading and parts of it are sold off as going concerns. In that case, although there might be nothing to be done with the existing company, you might be able to persuade the new one to treat you reasonably. See the next chapter, on changing employers, for information on this.

If there is no union, a law centre or Citizens Advice Bureau may be able to help you through the legal technicalities.

14 If your employer changes

This chapter covers your legal rights if the company is taken over, or the operation you are involved in is sold off or handed over to someone else. Protecting pensions in these circumstances involves two separate issues: safeguarding your past pension rights, and protecting your rights to build up pension for the future.

Currently, the law on protecting pension rights of people affected by a take-over is weaker than on many other items. The Transfer of Undertakings Regulations (TUPE) cover everything *except* occupational pensions. The Government has been consulting on proposals to change this, but it may be some time before the new rules come into effect. It has put forward several options, some more useful than others, and we do not yet know which one it will favour.

If the whole business changes hands, then the pension scheme as part of that business goes with it. There are some formalities concerning the arrangements for contracting out to be dealt with, but nothing else needs to change.

When only *part* of the business has changed hands – say, a particular factory or office – or where a contractor has taken on some of the tasks previously done by a firm and taken on the staff who had been carrying out that role as well, then keeping things as they are is not possible. The employees will need to be withdrawn from the old employer's pension scheme, as they are now working for a different employer. They can then legally be treated as early leavers from the old scheme.

The Inland Revenue will allow a 'period of grace' before the transfer takes place, but this is generally no more than six months. This is a very weak position, but there are some legal rays of light here:

▌ The European Court has been asked to rule on whether early retirement benefits due to be paid on redundancy are protected under TUPE, even if pensions generally are not. They gave one ruling, in the *Franklin* case, which suggested that since they were inextricably linked with the pension scheme as a whole, they were not protected. But they have been asked to look at the question further, in the *Beckmann* case.

■   Another case, *University of Oxford v Humphreys*, according to one lawyer, 'has been argued to give employees an opportunity to refuse to transfer and claim constructive dismissal by the original employer instead, if the benefits offered by the new employer will be less generous'.

■   In another recent case, *Howard Hagen and others v ICI Chemicals and others*, it was decided that ICI had been negligent. It had told the staff, whom it was trying to persuade to move as a block to a new employer, that their pensions would be 'equivalent', when in fact some were going to lose out. If the employees had known the true position, they would have been able to exert enough pressure on ICI to renegotiate the pensions element of the sale.

If you are in a GPP/stakeholder, and the current employer has given a contractual commitment to pay a contribution towards it, this may well carry over to the new employer under TUPE (because the exclusion only applies to *company* pensions). This has not yet been tested in court, however, so you might need to get legal advice if a case arose.

Moving from the public to the private sector

Where the government is selling something off, or outsourcing work to private contractors, it has committed itself to rather stronger protection. Before the final deal is done, the new employer has to offer the transferring staff 'broadly comparable' (but not identical) pension arrangements. In 'exceptional circumstances', where having a comparable scheme is not possible for some reason, compensation for the loss can be offered. No contract should be signed until agreement on pensions is reached, and the contract must include a specific requirement to put the new pension arrangements in place. This also applies to the health service and to other peripheral government bodies.

The Local Government Pension Scheme (LGPS) has some specific rules for people moving under the 'Best Value' arrangements. The

new employer can either transfer people into their 'broadly comparable scheme', or let them continue as members of the LGPS, under
an 'admission agreement'. If the contractor is providing its own
scheme it must also make a 'bulk transfer' agreement allowing staff
to transfer their past pension rights to the new scheme on the basis
of full service.

For more information, see _Staff Transfers in the Public Sector,_
available from the Cabinet office, or on its Web site at
www.cabinet-office.gov.uk/civilservice/2000/tupe/. For local
government, _The Pensions Implications of Transferring Employees to
an External Provider_ is available from the Local Government
Pensions Committee (LGPC). It's also available from its Web site,
www.lg-employers.gov.uk/pensions.html.

Before a takeover happens

The best time to influence what happens is before the transfer documents have been signed, when both old and new managements will
be anxious to reassure the workforce.

You and your fellow scheme members might want to consider
pressing the union on the following issues. If your employer has
been selling off or outsourcing pieces of work, and you think yours
might be next in line, find out from other ex-employees how they
have been treated. Look for a commitment from the company that
they will not finalize any sale without safeguarding the departing
employees' pension rights, both for the past and for the future.

Press both them and the trustees to commit themselves to paying
enough over as a bulk transfer to give the members full past service
credits. (This is called the 'past service reserve'.) Talk to the member
trustees and get them to press for this. Importantly, whatever agreement the _company_ makes does not bind the _trustees_, because they
have not signed it. The less that goes over to the new scheme as a
transfer value, the more will be left in the old scheme to reduce the
company's contributions or even give them a payment out. It is
clear in trust law, though, that the trustees are there to look after all
the members. You are still a member until the transfer has taken
place, so they should not favour one group over another.

As soon as you know who the new owners are, find out about
their pension arrangements. If the company is an acquisitive one,
which has been buying up other firms elsewhere, try to get in touch
with representatives there to find out what has happened with their
pensions.

Keep copies of any statements they make, or presentations that are given. Make notes of any meetings where pensions are discussed, and *keep* them even after things look as if they have been settled. You might even want to take a tape recorder to the crucial meetings.

If management are not making statements, ask them directly and try to pin them down in writing. Ask not just for general statements, but for specific information about what will happen to each person's benefits. Ask for a copy of the schedule to the sale-and-purchase agreement that covers pensions. You may not be able to get it officially, but if there is a mole in management, it could arrive in a brown paper envelope!

All this will be crucial if people have to take action to enforce whatever was agreed. It is only the members who have a real interest in doing this – so far as the old company is concerned, you will be ex-employees and of no interest.

What a good employer will do

The best safeguard for the members' benefits is for the new company to set up a 'facsimile' or 'mirror-image' scheme, with all the same benefits and powers for the trustees, and simply bring the members into it as if there had been no change. Next best is a 'broadly comparable' scheme, in the way the government actuary defines it (see above).

However, the new employer may not want to set up a complete new scheme, and may already have a scheme they want to offer you. They should provide a table of the differences between any offer and what you have now. It will be helpful to have an expert assessment, by an actuary (preferably with the company paying) of how big the differences are. A good rule of thumb is that in the *Hagen* case, discussed on page 150, the judge said that he regarded a difference of around 2 per cent as a significant gap.

Points to look out for particularly are:

■ Differences in the way pensionable salary is defined: are some elements of pay not pensionable now, where they were before, or vice versa? This will affect both the benefits and the contributions.
■ Differences in the early retirement rules: is the definition of ill health different, for instance?
■ Differences in the way dependants are treated: is there a pension for an unmarried partner in both cases, for instance?

If it is not possible to get an overall change, an alternative is some 'red-circling' of the people most badly affected – that is, that they stay on the same benefits as before, in money terms, until their wages rise enough for the differences not to matter. Another possibility is to get protection only for those in the last few years before retirement. If the new scheme's benefits are considerably worse than the scheme you are leaving, a good employer will provide financial compensation.

As for past service, the aim is to get full year-for-year credits (or more if the new scheme is not as good as the old) for those who transfer between two final-salary schemes. This will usually mean the right amount of money coming over as a 'bulk transfer value' from the old scheme. However, even if there is a shortfall on that, the union should try to obtain full credits – it is not your fault, after all, if the new employers have not been able to negotiate successfully with the previous trustees.

You and your fellow scheme members should try to avoid being rushed into agreeing a change before a deadline. You might be told, 'You have to agree to this because you cannot stay in your previous company's scheme beyond a certain date.' That's mainly for the convenience of that previous scheme, though, to get their administration out of their way. The IR does impose its own deadlines, but can be asked to extend them. If necessary you can start in the new company in a 'holding position' with the bare framework of a scheme set up while the details are still being discussed.

Scheme members will in due course have to make two different decisions: what to do about joining the scheme for the future, and what to do about transferring past service. Look back at Chapter 12 for some ideas on what to look for, and what advice and information people will need.

15 **If things go wrong**

The way in which complaints and grievances about your pension are dealt with depends on whether it is an occupational scheme, or a personal/stakeholder pension. It doesn't make any difference whether the occupational scheme is salary-related or money-purchase.

Occupational schemes

Internal disputes procedure

Every scheme must have a formal internal disputes procedure, in writing. A copy of this, along with the relevant forms, has to be given to anyone who is entitled to use it and asks for it. The disputes procedure must cover pension disputes between scheme members, potential members, and dependants and the scheme trustees. The personal representatives of deceased people in these categories may also complain. The trade union, or a friend or representative, can be authorized to assist with the complaint. There is no time limit for taking up cases, but the sooner you raise an issue the better, because documents will be more readily available and memories will be fresher.

Generally, scheme members are asked to raise queries with the Pensions Manager (or whoever else is appropriate) first, to see if they can be resolved simply, before putting them into the formal procedure. However, this must not be used as a way of blocking members from exercising their right to complain if they wish.

At the first formal stage, a complaint must be sent in writing to a 'nominated person' within the organization or external to it. An answer in writing should be given within two months, or an interim reply if a full one cannot be prepared in time. This reply must also explain the complainant's right to take the matter further.

As the second stage, there is the right to take the matter further within six months, to the Board of Trustees. Again the complaint must be in writing, with basic information about the issue, and must include a copy of the first-tier decision and an explanation of why the member disagrees. The trustees must then respond within two months, or send an interim reply.

OPAS and the Pensions Ombudsman

OPAS is an independent organization that can help people before a complaint starts, at any stage of their complaints, or if they are still not satisfied after they have gone through the disputes procedure. It can be contacted directly (see Appendix 4) or via a Citizens Advice Bureau.

Only a small proportion of all the queries it gets have to be taken further, with one of its advisers contacting the scheme. The rest are sorted out on the phone or by post. OPAS does not have legal powers itself, but it has a fairly high success rate, because problems it cannot solve are referred to the Pensions Ombudsman for investigation (explained below), and he *does* have legal powers. Very often, the fact of being able to say, 'Well, in a similar case recently the Ombudsman decided such-and-such' is enough.

The Pensions Ombudsman can deal with questions of maladministration, or disputes over fact or law. *Complaints* must be that 'the party complained against has behaved in a way which constitutes maladministration and that the maladministration has caused injustice'. *Disputes* can be disagreements concerning fact or law. They often arise alongside complaints of maladministration and do not usually need a separate investigation. *Maladministration,* the Ombudsman says, has been said to involve 'bias, neglect, inattention, delay, incompetence, ineptitude, perversity, turpitude, arbitrariness and so on'. It is not enough merely to disagree with a decision: the complainant must have reason to believe that the decision was not properly made or implemented. *Injustice* does not only mean financial loss – it may include distress, delay or inconvenience.

The Pensions Ombudsman has the power to enforce decisions through the courts. There is normally a three-year time limit on taking cases, but this means three years from the time when you became aware that there was a problem, and the Ombudsman has the power to waive the limit. He will usually treat time spent using the IDR procedure and/or being helped by OPAS as a good reason for delaying complaining to him.

The Ombudsman does not normally accept complaints for investigation unless they have been through the disputes procedure. However, if there is too much delay in responding to a complaint, or signs of deliberate foot-dragging, he does have the power to deal with it anyway. The cases that get to him are filtered through OPAS, but if a trade union or other body such as the Citizens Advice Bureau has already made efforts to resolve the issue, and explains this in the papers it sends in, OPAS will not bother to repeat the same steps before referring it on – though it might follow avenues that have not already been explored.

Some issues, in particular discrimination and equal treatment cases, and time off to carry out duties as a trustee, can either go to Employment Tribunals or down the OPAS/Ombudsman route.

After being blocked by the courts from dealing with 'class' actions, Section 54 of the Child Support, Pensions and Social Security (CSSSP) Act 2000 has given back to the Ombudsman the power to make representation orders and thus bind large groups of members, from April 2002 awards. The Pensions Ombudsman is also now allowed to investigate disputes between trustees of the same scheme (if referred to him by at least half the trustees), questions coming from a sole trustee, and complaints or disputes between statutory independent trustees and other trustees. In these cases, there is no need for the parties involved to allege that there has been any injustice.

There has been a steady decline in the proportion of cases upheld over the last few years, falling to a low of 39 per cent in 2000/01. This may be partly because more of the cases where the complainant clearly has a strong case are being settled before getting to the Ombudsman. There have been some quite significant victories for members as a result of complaints to the Ombudsman. The most notable was the *National Bus* case, where this Government has had to pay millions of pounds out to bus industry employees, after the Treasury grabbed the surplus in their pension fund during privatization of the industry under the Conservatives.

Going to court

Anyone who is not satisfied with the Pensions Ombudsman's decision can appeal to the High Court, and from there right up to the House of Lords, and a number of employers have done this where the Ombudsman's decision favoured the members. It is also possible to go to court directly, without following the Ombudsman route at all. The trust arrangement under which most pension schemes are set up, in theory allows any beneficiary, or potential beneficiary, to take the trustees to court for breach of trust. There is also the possibility of taking the employer to court for breach of their obligations.

The problem with taking the court route, however, is that the two parties – the claimant and the trustees – are not equally matched in terms of the resources they have behind them. At worst, the claimant is on his or her own, and could be running up debts as an individual, while the trustees are entitled to take the costs of a case from the fund. Whoever wins in a court case can demand that the other side pays their costs – and if the trustees have used top QCs in a case that has gone on for several days, these can be enormous. There have been cases in the past where the trustees have rather vindictively gone after individual claimants for costs they know they have no chance of meeting.

It is possible for claimants to get a court order, called a *Beddoes* order, which says that their costs too must come out of the fund, but their case must have a reasonable chance of success before the court will allow this. It is also possible to have 'friendly' litigation (though it tends to become increasingly unfriendly as the case goes on!) where the trustees agree to pay all the costs, in order to settle a point about the scheme on which there is genuine doubt. Taking a case to the Pensions Ombudsman for a ruling (as explained above) would be a cheaper route.

Before even threatening court action, it is important to get good legal advice. If you belong to a union, your union head office will be able to obtain this, but ask it to ensure that it comes from a specialist pensions lawyer (someone who is a member of the Association of Pension Lawyers). If the union thinks the case is strong enough, it will cover the costs. There have been occasions when the union has turned down the members and yet they have succeeded. For instance, in the *Hagen v ICI* case, discussed in Chapter 14, the members banded together and financed the action themselves. However, this should be the last resort. Other possible sources of advice, if you do not belong to a union, are a law centre or a Citizens Advice Bureau.

Action points

If you are not sure about your rights under the scheme, or how a benefit has been calculated, the OPAS helpline is staffed by experts and should be able to explain the position.

If you have a complaint about the pension scheme, try to get it resolved informally first, but if this is not possible, take it through the formal IDR procedure. If you belong to a union, it should be able to help with this, otherwise OPAS can do so.

The IDR is also a useful tool for dealing with collective issues if the employer will not negotiate on them; the group affected can all put in claims and ask for individual decisions. Keep tabs on your complaint once it goes into the procedure, to ensure that it is answered within the time limits. If all you are getting is a series of stalling letters, go to OPAS or the Ombudsman.

Member trustees who are in dispute with their fellow trustees may find it difficult to take the dispute to the Ombudsman, since they will need the support of half of the trustee board. However, they may be able to persuade the whole board that it is the best way of resolving a divisive issue. An alternative is for them to find scheme members who are affected by the dispute, and get some of them to put in test cases.

Keep all the correspondence and notes of any phone conversations or meetings where any issue seems likely to turn into a dispute. It's especially important that the union head office, law centre or a Citizens Advice Bureau gets to see the full picture (not just the points that support your argument!) when it is deciding whether to take things further.

Someone may need to 'whistleblow' to Opra in cases where it seems as if the pension scheme, or the employer, is not acting in line with the law. See below, for some points on this.

For further information, see the Opra leaflet *A Problem with your Company Pension?*, and the various bodies' Web sites, listed in Appendix 4. The Annual Reports published by OPAS and the Pensions Ombudsman give examples of cases from which people can learn. There is a detailed guide that would be useful for trustees, called *Pensions Disputes: Prevention and resolution*, edited by Jane Marshall (Jordans Publishers, 1998), and a subscriber Web site run by one of the City law firms that specializes in pensions: www.law-now.com/po-info/.

Personal and stakeholder pensions

The procedure for dealing with complaints here is rather fragmented, but if you take the wrong route, you should be told so, and put on the right road.

Your complaint might be against the way the employer is running your GPP or providing (or not providing) access to a stakeholder scheme. In that case, you would expect to take it up with the employer as with complaints about any other part of your working conditions, with your union's help or that of a law centre or

Citizens Advice Bureau if you do not belong to a union. (But see below about 'whistleblowing' to Opra.)

Alternatively, your complaint may be about the way the provider of the pension is acting. The provider must have a complaints procedure, which will usually include a form for you to fill in and send back. The Financial Ombudsman Service has some helpful hints about how to make a complaint:

▋ It's usually best to complain in writing. But if you phone, ask for the name of the person you speak to. Keep a note of this information, with the date and time of your call – and what was said. You may need to refer to this later.

▋ Try to stay calm and polite, however angry or upset you are. You're more likely to explain your complaint clearly and effectively if you can stay calm.

▋ If possible, start by contacting the person you originally dealt with. If he or she can't help, say you want to take matters further. Ask for details of the name or job title of the person who will be handling your complaint and for details of the firm's complaints details.

▋ When you write a letter of complaint, set out the facts as clearly as possible. This will make it easier for the firm to start putting things right.

▋ Write down the facts in a logical order and stick to what is relevant. Remember to include important details like your customer number or your policy or account number. Put these details at the top of your letter.

▋ Keep a copy of any letters between you and the firm. You may need to refer to it later.

If you're not happy with the firm's decision, then if it is a complaint about the sales and marketing of personal/stakeholder pensions, the Financial Ombudsman Service may be able to help (the address is in Appendix 4). You will need to fill in a complaint form, which you can obtain by phone or by downloading from the service's Web site.

If the problem is about the administration of the scheme, or with the employer rather than the provider, OPAS and the Pensions Ombudsman will deal with the issue. The procedure for taking a

case to them is the same as for occupational pensions, explained
above.

The Occupational Pensions Regulatory Authority

The Occupational Pensions Regulatory Authority (Opra) supervises occupational schemes and ensures that they comply with
certain parts of the Pensions Act 1995. It also now supervises some
parts of stakeholder pensions, and the payment of contributions to
all types of personal pensions. (Anything else to do with personal
pensions is supervised by the Financial Services Authority, FSA.)

Opra is set up in a rather strange way, as a 'reactive' regulator.
This means that it does not ask for an annual report from schemes,
or inspect them. Instead, it relies on the schemes themselves, or
their advisers, telling it when an occupational scheme has broken
the law, and the personal pension provider when the employer has
broken the law.

A pension scheme's actuary and auditor are required to contact
Opra if they have doubts about whether the scheme is complying
with the Pensions Act 1995 and this is called 'whistleblowing'.
Others, such as trustees or individual members, can also do so.

The staff will then investigate, and Opra can disqualify trustees,
order schemes to be wound up, and impose fines on trustees and
administrators for breaking the statutory requirements. It is also
able to fine *employers* who deduct pension scheme contributions
from the members' pay and then do not pass the money on to the
scheme (whether occupational or personal/stakeholder). This is by
far the most common problem that Opra has to deal with. The fines
for a first offence are small, but they can mount up for repeat
offences.

Opra publishes the names of the trustees or employers it penal-
izes, and a brief description of their offences, on its Web site.

Action points

If you think that the pension scheme, or the employer, may be
breaking the law, you can ring Opra's helpline (the number is
given at the end of this chapter) and discuss it without saying
what scheme it is. However, if you decide that someone must
'whistleblow', Opra warns that it may not be able to keep the
source of the complaint secret all the way through. The scheme's
advisers have legal protection. You can find out the name of the
actuary and auditor from the scheme's annual report, and you

could then telephone or write to them – anonymously if necessary – about your concerns. Alternatively, your union's full-time official or pensions officer, a law centre or a Citizens Advice Bureau would be able to pass on your concerns.

There is some legal protection for people who blow the whistle on their employers, in the Public Interest Disclosure Act 1998. An organization called Public Concern at Work can help with advice, but it is best to speak to it before rather than after taking action. Its address is in Appendix 4.

Further information

Opra's helpline, 01273 627600, is open during normal office hours. It publishes _Bulletins_ and a series of other (free) publications about different aspects of the law. Look at its Web site: www.opra.gov.uk.

Appendix 1

The Inland Revenue's rules

The IR lays down detailed rules about what pension schemes and providers must do if they want to be able to claim tax relief. These rules are different for occupational pension schemes and personal (including stakeholder) schemes. There are two large guidance manuals, called IR12 (for occupational schemes) and IR76 (for personal and stakeholder schemes); for details see Appendix 2. The IR likes to call the two types Chapter I and Chapter IV schemes, after the sections of the tax legislation that covers them.

These rules cover the *most* you can have or can pay. If you are trying to obtain improvements to a particular scheme, you need to assume they are written on tablets of stone. There is simply no point in asking for a spouse's pension of 75 per cent of the member's benefit, for instance, when the IR limits spouses' pensions in occupational schemes to 66 per cent.

The IR limits for occupational schemes (IR12)

For schemes approved under the occupational scheme rules, there are limits on both benefits and contributions. These limits are the same whether the scheme is final-salary, money-purchase, or hybrid.

What counts as earnings

Earnings of any type (basic, overtime, bonus, performance-related) can be pensionable. The taxable value of benefits in kind (like a company car) can also be taken into account. A scheme is allowed to use a different earnings formula for the pension and any life assurance benefit, provided that neither benefit goes over the limits.

However, for people who have changed their employer after June 1989, there is a 'cap' on the amount that can be counted for this purpose: £97,200 a year in 2002–03. It increases every April, more or less in line with the rise in the average earnings index.

The IR calls final pensionable salary 'final remuneration'. It can normally be calculated on the basis of your last year's earnings, or your earnings within the last 10 years before retirement, revalued to take account of price inflation. However, 'fluctuating emoluments' such as overtime may need to be averaged over three years, and there are special rules for the calculation of earnings for directors and very senior staff. These are all aimed at preventing people bumping up their pension in the last few years by working huge numbers of extra hours or giving themselves a quick promotion.

If someone has artificially low earnings in the last year before retirement, perhaps because they were off sick, the IR allows a 'notional' figure to be used for what they would have earned had things been normal.

How much pension?

The pension must not be more than two-thirds of 'final remuneration' in the last year before retirement, if the member has more than 20 years' service. This figure used to be 10 rather than 20 years, and those who joined before 1987 may still be able to take advantage of the old rule. If the scheme is contracted-in, you can have two-thirds on top of the full SERPS/S2P pension from the state.

They assume that people stay with the same employer for 40 years, so they will accept a 1/60th scheme without question. They will also accept a scheme with a higher accrual rate if it is not based on full earnings (for example, if the state pension is deducted from it – called 'integration' and explained in Chapter 2), or if the maximum service allowed is less than 40 years.

In calculating the two-thirds limit, you can ignore 'retained benefits' from a preserved pension with a previous scheme, *provided* that scheme was not 'better than 60ths'. So someone with a 1/50th scheme, for example, will need to have them taken into account. However, personal pensions and stakeholder pensions you have built up for yourself can be ignored.

How much cash?

Part of the pension can be turned into a tax-free lump sum, or the scheme can give one automatically. The most you can ever have as a lump sum in this way is either 1.5 times your final salary, or 2.25 times your pension, whichever is the greater.

Monica's earnings, in her last year before retirement, are £16,000. She has worked for the company for the full 40 years, and it is a 1/60th scheme.

To work out the maximum lump sum the IR would allow her to have, she needs to divide £16,000 by 80, then multiply by 3 and again by 40. So this means:

■ £16,000 divided by 80 = £200
■ £200 multiplied by 3 = £600
■ £600 multiplied by 40 = £24,000 – the amount she can take as a lump sum.

The alternative way of working it out is to start with her pension: 30/60ths of £16,000 is £8,000. Multiplying that by 2.25 gives her £18,000.

For the purpose of this calculation, you can use all your earnings plus the taxable value of benefits in kind (what the IR describes as 'remuneration').

Anyone who joined their pension scheme before 1989 may still be under the previous sets of IR limits. There are some special tax rules for people who joined between June 1987 and April 1989, but we will not cover the details of these as they cover very few people. Those who joined before June 1987 may find their scheme still has the earlier rules for the maximum limit. These say that:

■ anyone with 20 or more years' service can have 1.5 times their final earnings as a lump sum;

■ anyone with less than eight years' service can use the '3/80ths per year of service' formula;

■ for people with between nine and 19 years, the maximum depends on a table laid down by the IR. So for instance someone with 10 years' service can have 36/80ths, while someone with 19 years can have 108/80ths.

These maximum figures and rules are just the same for schemes that only give a lump sum and no pension, and those that give a lump sum on top of the pension.

The second question is how much you can 'sell' your pension for. A scheme can use a figure of £12 cash for every £1 given up, regardless of the member's age, so long as it does this for everyone.[1] If the scheme gives automatic pension increases, it can use higher figures for younger people, ranging down to £17.65 per £1 given up, for a woman aged 50, but the figures for those coming up to 65 will be lower in most cases. A scheme can actually *pay* more than this as a commutation rate, but it must use the IR's figures in calculating whether someone has hit the maximum or not.

You are allowed to turn the whole of a 'trivial' pension (less than £260 a year) into a lump sum. You will pay 20 per cent tax on the extra above what you would normally be entitled to take. The IR also allows schemes to commute the whole of the pension (except for the contracted-out element explained in Chapter 4), where someone is medically certified to be terminally ill and they are expected to live for less than a year.

It's important to understand how these different limits fit together. You are not allowed to have the maximum pension plus the maximum lump sum: the lump sum has to be deducted from the pension. The first calculation is always the pension. Any lump sum you get automatically is turned *back* into pension for the purpose of this calculation. So there is a check on whether your pension goes over the two-thirds limit first, and *then* a check on how much lump sum you can have.

When can you retire?

Every scheme must have a Normal Retirement Date (NRD) or more than one, which cannot normally be earlier than 50 or later than 75. The IR will allow an occupational scheme to have an NRD of anywhere between 60 and 70 without creating any problems. Some schemes, for particular occupations – like footballers, or ballet dancers – can have lower NRDs without asking special permission from the IR, but for any group not on its list, the employer would have to request it.

You are not allowed to take early retirement before the age of 50, except in cases of ill health. Under the current rules, the IR allows a scheme with an accrual rate of 1/60th or less to pay a pension of up to two-thirds of the member's final pensionable remuneration so long as the member has at least 20 years service.

However, if you joined before 1987, when the rules changed, and are in a scheme with an accrual rate *better* than 1/60th, you may be restricted by the 'N over NS' formula. This says that the benefit must be reduced in the same proportion as the actual number of years' service holds to the potential service. If someone has a potential working life with that employer of 40 years, but in fact retires after only 30, the maximum pension will be three-quarters of the ordinary maximum benefit. (This limit is not imposed, however, when early retirement is due to ill health.)

For voluntary early retirement, the pension can be calculated based on your actual years of service (and any credited entitlement). The years you could have worked up until NRD cannot be counted, but when you are going 'at the employer's request', or because of ill health, these extra 'prospective' years can be counted.

In a money-purchase scheme, the IR limit is the *greater* of 1/60th of final earnings for each year of service up to a maximum of 40, or the actuarial equivalent of the pension you would be entitled to at NRD.

Where the retirement is due to ill health, the pension can be based on all potential service up to normal retirement age, though on current earnings. A 'notional' figure can be used in the calculation, since the member's earnings may have been reduced due to illness. The IR definition of ill health is:

> physical or mental deterioration which is bad enough to prevent the individual from following his or her normal employment, or which seriously impairs his or her earning capacity. It does not mean simply a decline in energy or ability.

For *late* retirement, there are different maximum packages for those who joined their current scheme before 1 June 1989, and those who joined after that.

If you joined before 1 June 1989, you will have *continued rights* under the old rules. This means that the scheme can let you stay in the scheme for another five years (up to 70, or 65 if your scheme has an age 60 retirement age) and build up extra pension, to a maximum of 45/60ths. The lump sum can also be increased.

Alternatively, the scheme can freeze the pension at normal retirement age, and base it on your earnings then. It can then be increased either by an actuarial factor, or by the increase in the cost of living, whichever is the greater.

The scheme rules may also allow the individual the choice of drawing either the pension or the lump sum when they reach scheme retirement age, and then taking the other element when they do actually retire. If it is the pension element that is deferred, it can also be increased to take account of the time when the individual retires – but they are not allowed a second bite of the cherry in terms of extra lump sum.

If you joined after 1 June 1989, you are allowed to work on up to 75, but you don't have the option to take either the pension or the lump sum and carry on working; and you cannot increase your pension beyond the Inland Revenue's usual two-thirds limit by continuing to pay into it.

If someone dies in service after NRD, they can be given either the standard benefits for death in service, or the scheme can treat them as if they retired the day before their death.

Benefits paid on death

The maximum lump sum death benefit allowed is four times total PAYE earnings, and the taxable value of any benefits in kind. Schemes are allowed to use a 'notional' figure, by updating the last year's earnings by an amount to take account of inflation.

The cash sum is tax-free, so long as you fulfil the conditions laid down. The main one is that the scheme's trustees take the final decision about who gets the money. This means that at the point when you die, you do not own the money and so it is not part of your estate, as far as inheritance tax is concerned. Usually the scheme's administrator will ask a new member to fill in the nomination form or 'letter of wish' that is included in the scheme booklet. The trustees will follow this unless there is a particular reason not to.

The fund is allowed to hang on to the money, without deciding what to do with it, for up to two years. If it is still not paid after that, it must be transferred to an account outside the scheme. There is also a general legal rule that money left unclaimed after death, if it is still outstanding when sufficient time has been left after the settlement of a person's affairs, goes to the Crown. For this reason most scheme rules have a clause saying that the ultimate beneficiary, once the trustees have taken all reasonable steps to find someone to whom to pay the money, is the fund itself.

A scheme may also refund all the members' contributions on death, with the addition of a 'reasonable' rate of interest.

An employer is allowed to provide a lump sum death benefit alone, without offering any other sort of pension entitlement. So far as the law is concerned, this counts as an 'occupational pension scheme' so it is bound by the same rules as any other scheme.

Life assurance under any sort of pension policy must be what is called 'term assurance', ending when you start drawing your pension or leave. However, it is allowable to carry on providing it during early retirement due to ill health, and up to six months after a person leaves. The insurance company is also allowed to offer special terms if you want to continue your life assurance policy after you have left that employer, such as not requiring you to have a medical examination.

Spouses' and dependants' pensions

A scheme can provide a pension for a widow, widower or dependant, of up to two-thirds of the maximum pension the employee could have had if they had retired on grounds of ill health, on the date they died. This can include the pension equivalent of any separate lump sum retirement benefit that might have been paid. So all 'prospective' service can be used in the calculation and all earnings including the taxable value of benefits in kind, regardless of what the definition is for the member's own pension.

If there is both a spouse and dependants, more than one pension can be paid, so long as the total does not come to more than the member's own maximum pension.

Someone who has been living with the member as a 'common law husband / wife' or partner, may be able to qualify as a *dependant*. However, the IR says that:

> An unmarried partner, whether of the same or opposite sex, can qualify for a survivors pension only if he or she were financially dependent on the employee.... Financial interdependence of the employee... and his or her partner would be an acceptable criterion, e.g. where the partner relied on a second income to maintain a standard of living that had depended on joint income prior to the employee's... death.

So if two people are living together, even if one of them is paying the mortgage and the other is paying the milk bill, they will probably qualify as interdependent. If they were living apart, the trustees might need to ask for some evidence. The IR says that:

> Decisions on whether or not a person is dependent are a matter for the scheme trustees. IR SPSS would not challenge the trustees' judgement provided they had acted in accordance with the scheme rules.[2]

Children can always be regarded as dependent if they are under 18, or older if they are still in full-time education or training. A pension can be paid for life to a child who is disabled.

If the death occurs after retirement, the tax limits on the pension follow much the same pattern as for death in service – up to two-thirds of the maximum amount the member could have had as his or her own pension, with the balance available for a dependant's pension on top. The spouse's and dependant's pension can be calculated before any amount that has been commuted is deducted, so that taking part of the member's own pension as cash need not affect the spouse.

The IR will also allow up to £2,500 'bereavement' payment and a guarantee that the pension will be paid for a minimum length of time, which can be up to 10 years, even if the member dies in the meantime. If the guarantee is for five years or less, the balance may be taken as a lump sum. If it is for longer, it must be a continuing pension.

For anyone who joined his or her scheme before 1 October 1991, it is also possible for the lump sum death benefit coverage to continue into normal retirement. The cost of this has to be offset against the maximum pension that can be provided.[3]

You are allowed to surrender some of your own pension to increase the size of your spouse's pension, and to give a pension to any other dependant. However, this must not mean that the spouse's pension will be bigger than the member's own. The surrender must be done at, or shortly after, retirement, and cannot then be reversed. So if the dependant dies first, the sacrifice is wasted.

Increasing pensions

Once the pension starts being paid, it can be increased each year in line with the increase in the cost of living (the RPI), or by a fixed percentage, regardless of what the RPI is – but this fixed figure cannot be more than 3 per cent. If in the past the increases have been less than the RPI, or if the pension when it started was less than the maximum allowed under the other rules in this section, there can be extra increases in a 'catching up' exercise.

Contributions

A scheme member can contribute up to 15 per cent of total earnings, including the taxable value of benefits in kind in each tax year. This includes both the main scheme and additional contributions (AVCs). (Most people can contribute up to £3,600 a year to a personal/stakeholder scheme on top of this, as explained on page 121.)

There's no specific limit on how much the employer can put in, except in certain schemes for senior managers. However, the scheme must not be 'overfunded'.

If a member wants more money to go into the scheme, it is possible to arrange a 'sacrifice' of a salary increase, a bonus payment, or a redundancy payment and for the money to go to the scheme instead. However, all sacrifices over £5,000 pa must be reported to the district tax office to ensure that the sacrifice is an effective reduction in the employee's salary. The sacrifice must be done before the payment is made.

If you have a break in employment

If you are seconded to another employer, but have not joined their pension scheme, you can remain a full member of the original scheme so long as you expect to return to that employer in due course and thus continue to accrue pension. If you are absent without continuing to build up pension, you can remain a member of the scheme for up to 10 years, or indefinitely if the absence is because of sickness.

If the scheme breaks the tax rules

If the IR finds a scheme is not keeping to the rules, the penalties can be severe. In theory, the scheme can lose all tax relief, for the past as well as the future. In practice, the most the IR does is take away tax relief for a year at a time. But that is a severe enough penalty and would take some explaining to scheme members, so it happens very rarely. There are cases, though, where someone discovers they have an unexpected tax bill, perhaps because they have been given a bigger lump sum on retirement than they should have been.

How you get the tax relief

Tax relief on occupational pensions is given 'at source', which means that your pension contribution is deducted from your pay *before* PAYE is taken off. This means that your tax bill is less than it might otherwise be. For example, a woman is on £300 a week, and pays £15 a week pension contribution. So this is deducted, leaving £285. Her PAYE tax is then calculated as if she had earned only £285.

If you are on the basic rate of tax, then for every £1 you pay into your pension scheme, you save 22p tax. If you are on the 40 per cent rate, then for every £1 you put in you save 40p.

Tax limits for personal pensions (IR76)

For pensions covered by the Personal Pension tax rules, the limits are on the contributions rather than the benefits, and they apply to employer and employee contributions added together. Anyone, whatever their earnings (or even if they have no earnings at all) can put in up to £3,600 a year. If you want to put in more than that, up to the age of 35, the maximum is 17.5 per cent of earnings. For older people, it is:

Age	per cent
36–45	20
46–50	25
51–55	30
56–60	35
61–74	40

There is a 'cap' on the earnings that can be counted as pensionable (£95,400 from April 2001–02).

Earnings on which the contributions are based can be all those on which you are taxed. You nominate a particular tax year as the 'basis year'. This can be either the current one, or any of the previous five, and this then gives you a contribution limit for this tax year. You can continue to use this same 'basis year' for any of the next five years, or you can move forward to another one that gives you a better result.

You can pay into more than one personal pension at a time, including stakeholder schemes, so long as you don't go above the top limits when the contributions are added together.

You pay contributions out of your net (take-home) pay. The personal pension provider then collects a refund of basic-rate tax from the IR. A higher-rate taxpayer has to make a claim for the additional refund on the rest.

You can start to draw the pension at any age between 50 and 75, whether you have stopped working or not. You can draw 25 per cent of your fund as a tax-free lump sum. (This rule has only existed in its present form since 1986, and those who had the older form of PP – usually called a Section 226 policy – can still be covered by the slightly more generous earlier limits.)

Rather than turn the rest of the fund into an annuity (a pension bought from an insurance company) immediately, it is possible to start by taking money directly out of the fund. This is called an 'income withdrawal' or 'drawdown' scheme. You must buy an annuity, however, by the time you reach 75.

You can have life insurance (death benefit) with a personal pension, but the rules have changed recently on how much you can spend on this, and still get tax relief. If you took the policy out any time before 5 April 2001, if you buy life assurance within a personal pension scheme, you can have tax relief on premiums of up to 5 per cent of the total pensionable earnings – as part of the overall limits, not as an addition to them. For contracts made after 6 April 2001, however, the maximum that can be paid towards life assurance will be 10 per cent of the contribution, which is generally going to be much less.

Anyone already paying for life assurance under the previous rule, *or* with an option to do so in his or her pension contract, can continue without any change. It is only when they start a new pension contract that they will be bound by the new rule.

The insurance companies are responsible to the IR for keeping to the limits. If by mistake they take more contributions than you are allowed to pay in, they will have to pay back the tax relief they have got, and return your contributions to you.

Notes

1. Pensions Update 80.
2. IR12, Glossary.
3. Pensions in Practice, p 119.

Appendix 2

Further reading

Books, guides and bulletins

Capita, *Annual Pension Scheme Administration Survey*, London

Child Poverty Action Group, *Welfare Benefits Handbook*, published annually, Child Poverty Action Group, London

Incomes Data Services (2001) *Pensions in Practice*, Incomes Data Services, London

Inland Revenue (2001) *Occupational Pension Schemes Practice Notes*, *(IR12, 2001)*

Inland Revenue (2001) *Personal Pension Scheme Guidance Notes (including Stakeholder Pensions) IR76*

Marshall, J (1998) (ed) *Pensions Disputes: Prevention and resolution*, Jordans Publishers, Bristol

NAPF, *Disclosure Made Simple*, National Association of Pension Funds, London

NAPF, *Survey of Occupational Schemes*, published annually, National Association of Pension Funds, London

Opra, *A Problem with Your Company Pension?*, free; Tel: 01273 627600

Opra, *Bulletins*, issued every two months, are free from Opra, Tel: 01273 627600, or on its Web site: www.opra.gov.uk

Opra, *Guide for Pension Scheme Trustees*, free, Tel: 01273 627600

Opra, *Paying Pension Contributions on Time: A guide for employers with occupational pension schemes*, free; Tel: 01273 627600

Pensions Management Institute/PRAG (1997) *Pensions Terminology*, fifth edition, explains the terms used in UK pensions. These have been largely standardized, though you may still find some scheme-specific jargon being used

Pensions Research Accountants Group (PRAG) (1996) *Financial Reports of Pension Schemes: A statement of recommended practice*

Self, R (1998) *Pension Fund Trustee Handbook*, Tolley, London

TUC (2000) *Your Rights at Work*, Kogan Page, London

Ward, S (2001) *Pensions Handbook*, Age Concern Books, London

Ward, S (forthcoming) *Changing Direction*, Age Concern Books, London

Magazines

IDS Pensions Service Bulletin (10 times a year), 193 St John Street, London EC1V 4LS. Subscribers also receive copy of *Pensions in Practice*

Occupational Pensions (monthly), 18–20 Highbury Place, London N5 1QP

Pensions Management (monthly), Greystoke Place, Fetter Lane, London EC4A 1ND

Pensions Week (weekly), Maple House, 149 Tottenham Court Road, London W1P 9LL

Pensions World (monthly), 2 Addiscombe Road, Croydon, Surrey CR9 5AF

Professional Pensions (weekly), Thames House, 18 Park Street, London SE1 9ER

TUC publications

Getting the Best from Defined Contribution Schemes (1997) jointly produced by the TUC and Union Pensions Services, this guide explains how these schemes work and how unions can get the best deal for their members.

Pension Fund Investment: A TUC handbook (1996) a comprehensive guide to all aspects of pension fund investment with action points for trustees. Takes account of the changes resulting from the 1995 Pensions Act.

Pensions for Women – a TUC guide (2001) this new guide to

pensions options for women includes all the latest information on stakeholder pensions and other opportunities for women who want to save for their retirement.

Shareholder Voting – A guide for member trustees (1998) produced by the TUC in association with PIRC. Gives advice on corporate governance and model guidelines on how pension funds ought to approach the formal business dealt with at company AGMs.

TUC Pensions Briefing, contains current pension issues / concerns, articles from Pensions Officers and others, information about training courses, government reviews, etc. The TUC Member Trustees Network provides services tailored specifically for member nominated trustees, including trustees newsletter (to be re-launched in 2002), trustee training, guidance notes on being a trustee and information about pension fund investment.

Appendix 3

Courses and conferences

TUC Pension Courses are for anyone involved in pensions. Several unions and the GFTU also run courses for pension trustees, but the big providers are the NAPF and the commercial firms of consultants. Their courses are quite good, but tend to be biased towards the employer rather than the member viewpoint.

The Northern Pensions Conference, held in Newcastle upon Tyne in July each year, is a major annual event for member-trustees and union activists. Contact Sue Ward, 5 Goldspink Lane, Newcastle upon Tyne NE2 1NQ.

The Pensions Management Institute (PMI, 4–10 Artillery Lane, London E1 7LS) runs examinations for a 'Certificate of Essential Pension Knowledge' and courses leading to this are run by a number of providers. You can work through the syllabus in your own time by using the computer package provided by Aries (11 Lever Street, London EC1V 3QU, Tel: 020 7490 5440). A number of unions and consultants subscribe to this and so can provide you with copies at a cheaper rate – ask them first.

Appendix 4

Useful addresses

Government bodies and quangos

Disability Rights Commission
DDA Information
Freepost MIDQ2164
Stratford upon Avon
CV37 9BR
Information line: 0345 622633, or textphone: 0345 622644; Web site:
www.drc-gb.org

Employment Tribunals Service
Helpline: 0845 795 9775; Minicom users: 0845 757 3722; Web site:
http://www.ets.gov.uk
Claim forms and other information about taking a claim.

Equal Opportunities Commission (EOC)
Overseas House
Quay Street
Manchester M3 3HN
Tel: 0161 833 9244; Web site: www.eoc.org.uk/

Financial Ombudsman Service (FOS)
South Quay Plaza
183 Marsh Wall
London E14 9SR
Tel: 0845 080 1800; Web site: www.financial-ombudsman.org.uk
Helps consumers resolve complaints about most personal finance
matters. The service is independent, and free for consumers.

Financial Services Authority (FSA)
25 The North Colonnade
Canary Wharf
London E14 5HS
Tel: 020 7676 1000; Public enquiries: 0845 606 1234; Web site:
http://www.fsa.gov.uk/
The regulator for most forms of investment.

Inland Revenue, Savings, Pensions, Share Schemes (SPSS)
Yorke House
PO Box 62
Castle Meadow Road
Nottingham NG2 1BG
Tel: 0115 974 1600
Grants tax approval for occupational pension schemes and moni-
tors them to ensure that they do not break the rules for tax relief.

National Insurance Contributions Office
Benton Park Road
Longbenton
Newcastle upon Tyne NE98 1YX
Tel: 0191 213 5000; Web site: http://www.inlandrevenue.gov.uk
Deals with National Insurance contribution records and payments.
Part of the Inland Revenue.

Office of the Pensions Advisory Service (OPAS)
11 Belgrave Road
London SW1V 1RB
Tel: 020 7233 8080; Web site: http://www.opas.org.uk
A voluntary organization that gives advice and information on
occupational and personal pensions and helps sort out problems.

Occupational Pensions Regulatory Authority (Opra)
Invicta House
Trafalgar Place
Brighton BN1 4DW
Tel: 01273 627600; Web site: http://www.opra.gov.uk and
http://www.stakeholder.opra.gov.uk
Responsible for regulating occupational pension schemes under
the Pensions Act 1995. Also responsible for registering and super-
vising stakeholder schemes.

Pensions Ombudsman
11 Belgrave Road
London SW1V 1RB
Tel: 0207 834 9144; Web site: http://www.pensions-ombudsman.org.uk
Deals with complaints or disputes about occupational and personal pension schemes. Appointed by the government.

Pensions Registry
PO Box 1NN
Newcastle upon Tyne NE99 1NN
Tel: 0191 225 6437
Will trace the address of a pension scheme with which you have lost touch, so that you can find out whether you have a pension due.

The Pensions Service
The DWP's new name for the unified service dealing with all pensioner matters. Contact details are not yet available, but Web site is www.thepensionservice.gov.uk.
Other useful DWP Web sites are www.gogetpensions.gov.uk, www.info4pensioners.gov.uk, and www.pensionguide.gov.uk.

Public Concern at Work
Public Concern at Work
Suite 306
16 Baldwins Gardens
London EC1N 7RJ
Helpline: 020 7404 6609
Web site: http://www.pcaw.co.uk

Public Concern at Work (Scottish Office)
Wellpark Enterprise Centre
120 Sydney Street
Glasgow G31 1JF
Helpline: 0141 550 7572
An independent charity that seeks to ensure that concerns about malpractice in the workplace are properly raised and addressed.

Trade and professional organizations

Association of Consulting Actuaries
1 Wardrobe Place
London EC4V 5AH
Tel: 020 7248 3163; Web site: www.aca.org.uk
Professional body for actuaries who work as consultants.

Association of Pension Lawyers
Tel: 020 7667 7216; Web site: http://www.apl.org.uk
An organization for lawyers who work on pensions.

Institute of Actuaries
Staple Inn Hall
High Holborn
London WC1V 7QJ
Tel: 020 7242 0106; Web site: http://www.actuaries.org.uk
Professional body for actuaries.

National Association of Pension Funds (NAPF)
NIOC House
4 Victoria Street
London SW1H 0NX
Tel: 020 7808 1300; Web site: www.napf.co.uk
Represents occupational pension funds.

Pensions Management Institute
4–10 Artillery Lane
London E1 7LS
Tel: 020 7247 1452; Web site: http://www.pensions-pmi.org.uk
Aims to promote high professional standards in the pensions industry; the major examining board for pension qualifications.

Glossary of terms and abbreviations

Note. This glossary is partly taken from the Plain English Campaign's A–Z of Pensions, with their permission, with some additions and amendments, which have asterisks beside them. The A–Z is available on the Campaign's Web site, www.plainenglish.co.uk, and it can be contacted at PO Box 5, New Mills, High Peak SK22 4QP.

Accrual rate　In a defined benefit scheme this is the rate at which pension benefits build up for the member. They will get a certain amount for each year of pensionable service.

Actuarial valuation*　This is an assessment done, usually every three years, by the actuary to work out what money needs to be put into the scheme in the future to ensure that the pensions can be paid.

Actuary　An actuary is an expert on pension scheme assets and liabilities, life expectancy and probabilities (the likelihood of things happening) for insurance purposes. An actuary works out whether enough money is being paid into a pension scheme to pay the pensions when they are due.

Additional pension　This is what the government sometimes calls the pension paid by SERPS.

Additional voluntary contribution (AVC)*　This is an extra amount (contribution) a member can pay to his or her own pension scheme to increase the future pension benefits.

Annuity　This is a fixed amount of money paid each year until a particular event (such as death). It might be split into more than one payment, for example monthly payments.

Many schemes use an annuity to pay pensions. When someone retires, his or her pension scheme can make a single payment, usually to an insurance company. This company will then pay an annuity to the member. The money paid to the member is what people usually call their pension.

Annuity rate   This compares the size of an annuity (how much it pays each year) with how much it cost to buy.

APP   Appropriate Personal Pension.

AVC   Additional Voluntary Contribution.

Basic pension   This is what the government sometimes calls the basic state pension.

Basic state pension   This is a pension paid by the government to people who have enough qualifying years. It is not earnings related.

Beneficiaries   These are the people who are paid money, or might be paid in the future, from a pension scheme. For example, there is the individual who is actually paying in to the scheme, and also his or her spouse and children who will be paid money if the member should die before they do.

Benefit statement   This is a statement of the pension benefits a member has earned. It may also give a prediction of what his or her final pension might be.

Benefits   With pension schemes, this is everything the members get after retiring because they were part of the scheme. It usually means the money paid to the members as their pension. It could also include death benefits.

   With insurance, this is the money the insurance firm pays out if something happens. For example, a life assurance policy would pay death benefits if the insured person dies.

Buy out policy*   This is an insurance policy that pension scheme trustees can buy for a member instead of paying him or her pension benefits. The insurance company will pay the member (or the member's dependants) a pension, either immediately or when it becomes due.

COMP   Contracted Out Money Purchase.

Contracted out   This term is used to describe a scheme where the members contract out of SERPS.

Contributions   This is the money paid into a pension fund for a member. It can be paid by a member or an employer.

COSR   Contracted Out Salary Related (pension scheme).

DB   Defined Benefits.

DC   Defined Contribution.

Deferred pension*   This is a pension left in a pension scheme, when someone stops being a member.

Defined benefit scheme   This is where the rules of the scheme decide how much pension the member will get. There are different ways of working out the size of the pension, but the member will know which system the scheme uses. The most common type of defined benefit scheme is a final-salary scheme.

Defined contribution scheme   This is where the size of the member's pension is not decided by the rules of the scheme. The size of the member's pension will be affected by how much money is put into the pension fund for the member, how much the pension fund has grown, and what annuity rate is available when the member retires. This system is also called a money-purchase scheme.

DSS   Department of Social Security (now DWP).

DWP   Department of Work and Pensions.

Earnings cap*   This is a limit on how much of a member's earnings is allowed to be used to work out the limits on contributions and benefits in an approved scheme. This limits the amount that a high earner can put into a pension scheme and still get tax relief.

EPB   Equivalent Pension Benefits (*see* page 4).

Free-standing additional voluntary contributions (FSAVCs)*   These are extra contributions that members can pay into arrangements outside their own pension scheme to increase their pensions.

FRS17*   This is the 'financial reporting standard' followed by auditors, when they decide what figures to give for the cost of pensions in a company's accounts. For a defined-contribution scheme, it is simply the contributions made. For a defined-benefit scheme, the auditor has to decide whether more or less has been paid into the scheme than was needed at the time, and allow for this in the figures that are used. One effect is that if the company gives the workers better pension benefits, the costs will mean that the company's profits are reduced for that year.

Funding*   This means setting aside money now, to pay for pensions in the future. The contributions are invested, so that the future income can be added to the fund and increase what is available.

GMP   Guaranteed Minimum Pension.

GPP   Group Personal Pension.

Graduated pension scheme   This was an additional state pension that was building up before 5 April 1975.

Group personal pension (GPP)*   This is a system where several employees at one company join a personal pension scheme with the same pension firm. Each member has a separate policy with the pension firm, but contributions are collected by the employer and passed on.

Guaranteed minimum pension (GMP)   A member of a contracted out occupational pension scheme will get at least this much pension unless:
- the member's service is all after 5 April 1997. His or her benefits would then come under limited price indexation (LPI);
- some of the member's service is after 5 April 1997. He or she would have some of the benefits affected by GMP and some by LPI;
- the scheme is a contracted out money-purchase scheme. The member's benefits are then affected by Protected Rights.

IB   Incapacity Benefit.

Income drawdown (withdrawal)   This is when a member retires, but chooses not to buy an annuity straightaway. Until the member buys an annuity, he or she takes an income from the scheme.

IP   Income Protection.

IR   Inland Revenue.

JSA   Job Seeker's Allowance.

LGPS   Local Government Pension Scheme.

Lower earnings limit (LEL)*   This is the least amount someone must earn before he or she starts to build up benefits in the National Insurance system.

LPI   Limited Price Inflation.

MIG   Minimum Income Guarantee.

Minimum Funding Requirement (MFR)*   This is a set of rules laid down by the Government in the Pensions Act 1995, for how much money a final earnings scheme must have in it to pay for the benefits that have been promised. The calculations are done by the *actuary*, on the basis of a standardized set of assumptions. The MFR has not worked very well, and the Government plans to abolish it.

MND   Member Nominated Director.

MNT   Member Nominated Trustee.

Money-purchase scheme   This is where the size of the member's pension is worked out by the money-purchase method. The size of the member's pension will be affected by how much money is put into the pension fund for the member, how much the pension fund has grown, and what annuity rate is available when the member retires. This is also called a *defined contribution scheme*.

NAPF   National Association of Pension Funds.

National Insurance   This is money that the government takes from both workers and employers. The amount depends on how much the worker earns. Some government benefits, such as the basic state pension and SERPS, depend on how much National Insurance you have paid.

NRD   Normal Retirement Date.

OPRA   Occupational Pensions Regulation Authority.

Personal pension   This is someone's personal pension arrangement. It can also mean a retirement annuity set up before July 1988.

PHI   Permanent Health Insurance.

PP   Personal Pension.

Protected Rights   This is the lowest amount of benefits that a contracted out money-purchase scheme (COMPS) can pay to a member. This amount is worked out by using the money-purchase method with the money paid into the scheme as minimum contributions or minimum payments.

RPI   Retail Prices Index.

Salary-related scheme   This is a scheme where the member's pension depends on his or her earnings. It is a type of *defined benefit scheme*.

Section 32 annuity   Also called a 'Section 32 policy', this is another name for a *buy out policy*.

SERPS   *see* State Earnings Related Pension.

Stakeholder*   A stakeholder scheme is a sort of personal pension, which has to meet certain conditions such as how the scheme is run and what charges it makes.

State earnings related pension scheme (SERPS)*   This is the extra state pension that employed people could earn up to 5 April 2002. They paid extra National Insurance contributions once their earnings reached the lower earnings limit. People could choose to contract out of SERPS by joining an appropriate occupational or personal pension scheme.

State second pension (S2P)*   This is what the Government replaced the SERPS scheme with in April 2002. It has been designed so that people who do not earn a lot should get a higher pension than they would have done with SERPS.

Transfer value (TV)   This is the amount paid as a transfer payment.

Trustee   This is a person or a company appointed to carry out what the trust must do. They must follow the laws that apply to trusts.

TUC   Trades Union Congress.

Unit linked pension   In this type of pension scheme the pension scheme benefits depend on what happens to a unitized fund. The scheme is usually linked to the unitized fund through an insurance policy.

Upper earnings limit (UEL)   This is the highest amount of earnings on which employees pay National Insurance. The employer still pays National Insurance for earnings above this limit.

USS   Universities Superannuation Scheme.

WGMP   Widow's Guaranteed Minimum Pension.

With-profits policy   This is a type of insurance policy. It means that a policyholder will get a share of any surplus in the insurance company's life insurance and pensions business.

Index